THREE-DIMENSIONAL APPLIQUÉ

and

EMBROIDERY EMBELLISHMENT

TECHNIQUES FOR TODAY'S ALBUM QUILT

by

Anita Shackelford

American Quilter's Society

P. O. Box 3290 • Paducah, KY 42002-3290
www.AQSquilt.com

Located in Paducah, Kentucky, the American Quilter's Society (AQS) is dedicated to promoting the accomplishments of today's quilters. Through its publications and events, AQS strives to honor today's quiltmakers and their work and to inspire future creativity and innovation in quiltmaking.

Library of Congress Cataloging-in-Publication Data

Shackelford, Anita
    Three-dimensional appliqué & embroidery embellishment : techniques
for today's album quilt.
            p.   cm.
    Includes bibliographical references (p. 147) and indexes.
    ISBN 1-57432-823-9 : $24.95
        1. Appliqué--Patterns.   2. Quilting--Patterns. 3. Embroidery-
-Patterns.   4. Album quilts.   I Title.   II Title: Three
-dimensional appliqué and embroidery embellishment.
TT779.S43   1994
746.44'5--dc20   93--48425
                                                                           CIP

Additional copies of this book may be ordered from:

American Quilter's Society
P.O. Box 3290 • Paducah, KY 42002-3290
1-800-626-5420 (orders only)
or visit our website at www.aqsquilt.com

Copyright: 1994, 2003, Anita Shackelford
Photography by Richard Walker

▷ *Spring At Last!* 1992, 28"x 28" Made by the author.
Rich reds, blues, and purples of a fabric challenge issued by the Gatherings of Quilters in Toledo, Ohio inspired this basket of spring flowers. Techniques include padded and corded appliqué, surface quilting, ruching, and embroidery. In the collection of Mary Andra Holmes, Phoenix, AZ.

ACKNOWLEDGMENTS

No one works alone. Many people have helped lay the groundwork for this book and to them I am truly grateful.

To my family for giving me the time to create and to share my work with others. Especially to my husband, Richard, for always encouraging me to grow, to be more tomorrow than I am today.

To my aunt, Virginia Reiff, for putting the needle in my hand so many years ago.

To Lois K. Ide for sharing techniques learned from her mother and for encouraging me to trust my own creative abilities.

To my good friends who have worked with me through the past five years, shared their insights and talents as we developed new ideas, and always asked for more: Glenda Clark, Janet Hamilton, Sheila Kennedy, JoAnn Lischynski, Joan Longbrake, Dorothy McAdam, Rebecca Whetstone.

To Bill and Meredith Schroeder for giving me the opportunity to share my work through the American Quilter's Society shows, American Quilter magazine, Museum of the American Quilter's Society (MAQS), and this book.

To Victoria Faoro, Elaine Wilson, and Whitney Hopkins at AQS

To Richard Walker, Schenevus, NY, photographer

To Helen Hansen and Jean Gardner at the Follett House Museum in Sandusky, Ohio for allowing me to study their magnificent album quilt and share it with you.

To my students all across the country who have enjoyed my workshops and encouraged me to put it all in writing.

TABLE OF CONTENTS

◁ *Follett House Quilt. One block from the antique quilt that inspired the author.*

INTRODUCTION

I have been making quilts since the late 1960's and feel as if I have been in love with quilts all of my life. There is something magical and very satisfying about combining color and texture to create new work. I have made quilts in many styles, but when I look back at my work, my best quilts have always been appliqué. I find appliqué's floral themes and freedom of design especially appealing. I am a nature lover, following the seasons with my garden, the birds and other creatures, and the farmlands that surround me. I love being able to translate these ideas into cloth – to make my quilts a reflection of how we live our lives.

My first introduction to the high art of mid-nineteenth century appliqué was at the Firelands Association for the Visual Arts in Oberlin, Ohio in 1983. On display was an album quilt belonging to the Follett House Museum in Sandusky, Ohio. It is a masterpiece of dimensional work, full of ruching, stuffed work, and fine detail. By studying the work done on antique quilts and sharing ideas with others who were familiar with this type of work, I was able to incorporate some of those techniques into the traditional patterns that were available at the time.

When I began to design my own work, I found that I also had to develop new ways to produce the embellishments for a more realistic look. Over the last five years, I have experimented, quietly alone in my studio and not so quietly with a group of friends, to develop and perfect the techniques that I share with you here.

The focus of this book is on adding dimension and fine detail to appliqué work. The techniques themselves are not new, having been taken from nineteenth century album quilts. By studying the basic techniques and then adapting them to achieve what I wanted, I have translated these ideas into more contemporary designs.

This book is set up as a progressive workbook, concentrating on dimensional techniques and embellishments rather than large patterns. Each section includes general discussion of a particular technique, along with helpful hints to make the work go more smoothly and solve some problems before they happen. You may study the techniques and file them away for future reference, or work through the book and practice each one on a small scale. I have designed a 6" block to provide a practice piece for each technique. Full size patterns for these blocks can be found at the end of the book. If you want to finish the blocks, they may be set together into a sampler quilt of any size.

Although these blocks are small, I found that I was not able to create a design without combining several techniques and embellishments. Therefore, along with a pattern and instructions for the main technique, you will find notations for the elements completing the block. You may refer to each section as needed to finish the design, or add to the block as you progress through the book.

Once the techniques have been learned, I hope that you will incorporate them into existing patterns, or use them to create new work. The gallery section shows additional new pieces which have been made using these dimensional techniques.

I have made notations for metric measurements for those who are more comfortable working in that system. The measurements may not always reflect accurate conversions, but they are measurements that are easily obtained and will work.

If you are left handed, you will find areas of instructions written especially for you.

There are many different approaches to preparing pieces for appliqué and stitching them into place. If you have picked up this book, chances are you have done some appliqué and are comfortable with the process. Use whatever technique works best for you. There are many good books available on the subject of hand appliqué and I have not repeated much basic instruction here. If you need help, ask at your local quilt shop or check the reference section at the back of the book.

APPLIQUÉ
BASICS

PREPARATION

FABRICS

My first choice in fabrics is 100% cotton. I look for quality fabrics with a good thread count and a soft hand. When using blend fabrics you will often have problems with raveling and shadow-through. Blends do not hold a crease as well either, making it more difficult to turn seam allowances.

The type of prints chosen for the quilt depends on the look you are trying to achieve. For example, multicolored calicos will give you a country look, while a quilt of all solid colors can be very dramatic. A classic look will include a variety of prints and solids. You may want to study pic-tures of antique quilts to see which you prefer. I tend to use monochromatic (one color) prints. They have visual texture, but do not have other colors in them, which I sometimes find spotty and distracting. Often these monochromatic prints will have a good solid color on the back, which gives me another perfectly coordinated fabric choice.

Fabrics can be chosen for their visual texture and used to represent a specific item or material. You may find prints that look like wood grain, marble, basket weave, etc. Shaded leaves, fruits, and flowers can be cut from bold prints. Birds and butterflies might be found and used *broderie perse* style.

I pre-wash every fabric that I use, to remove the sizing and to guard against colors bleeding later.

GRAIN

Most sources recommend that the grain line of an appliqué piece should match the grain of the background block. If you are working with large pieces and cutting out behind them, a consistent grain line will help to stabilize the block. Most of my work is designed to a delicate scale with hundreds of pieces going in all directions. Besides running the risk of losing my mind trying to match grain lines, I actually think it is important *not to*. I have always cut my pieces for appliqué off grain. Because bias will stretch, it requires a little care in handling, but cutting pieces off grain can also be used to your advantage. The shading that develops as the light falls on changing grain lines adds to the visual texture of appliquéd flowers and leaves. From a practical standpoint, I find that the softer bias edges are easier to turn and do not ravel. Deep inner notches and curves which need to be clipped seem to have fewer stray threads to control when those edges are on the bias. Cut on the bias, a large flat piece such as a vase can adjust itself to lie flat, even if it is not perfectly sewn. I was surprised, and then a little amused, to see that the vases in the Follett House quilt had been cut on the bias. The woman who made this quilt knew this secret 150 years ago.

TEMPLATES

I have worked with a variety of template materials – plastic, freezer paper, architect's vellum, and X-ray film to name a few. Paper is quick for templates that I don't intend to keep, while the sturdier materials may be reused many times. Templates for appliqué should be made the size of the piece to be appliquéd, with no seam allowance added. Simply place the template material over the pattern, trace the motif, and cut out the template on the drawn lines.

Most of the time, I prefer to draw around templates on the fabric and use the marked line as a guide for turning the seam allowance. To mark outlines, place the template right side up on the right side of the material and draw around it. There are many other options, including freezer paper on top or underneath, or simply turning the seam allowance by eye. I have used most of them at one time or another,

depending on the situation. Use the one that works best for you.

One of the most commonly asked questions in workshops is about choosing a marker. A wide variety of marking pencils and tools are available. It is important to me that no marks show on a finished piece so I look for those that are easily removed. Berol® Verithin® white and silver pencils show up well on most fabrics and generally come off in the handling of the piece. Chalk markers or pencils also make a highly visible line that will brush off. The Berol® Karismacolor® Graphite Aquarelle is a soft dark pencil that makes marks that are easily removed, sometimes in the handling, or by erasing or washing. Be sure to test the marker that you plan to use *on the fabric that you plan to use*, as each one may react differently.

CUTTING

When cutting out an appliqué shape, add ³⁄₁₆" (.5 cm) allowance all around, to be turned under when the piece is appliquéd down. Don't worry if your cutting line is not absolutely uniform. It is the drawn outline that will determine the final shape of the piece.

CLIPPING

Concave or inner curves will require a little give in their seam allowances in order for them to turn under smoothly. A gentle curve cut on the bias may stretch enough, but most will need to be clipped. A series of small cuts, perpendicular and almost to the finished outline, will allow the seam allowance to fan out when it is turned. (Fig. 1) Deep notches will need just one cut made straight into the notch, to within a thread or two of the turn line. (Fig. 2) Again, a bias edge here will make this easier to control because it will not ravel.

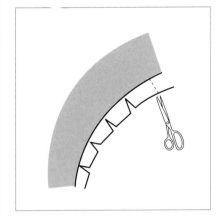

△ *Fig. 1. Clip seams on a concave curve.*

△ *Fig. 2. Clip straight in on a deep notch.*

◁ *Follett House Quilt.* One block from the antique quilt that inspired the author.

BASTING & NEEDLE TURN TECHNIQUES

Appliqué pieces may be sewn down using needle turn or pre-basted edges. Since most of my work is layered, I prefer to have pieces basted to finished size in order to judge their placement in relation to one another.

If you want to pre-baste the seam allowance under, hold the piece in your hand with the right side toward you so that you can see the drawn outline. Turn the edge away from you and secure it in place with a running stitch. Follow the drawn line *exactly* in order to achieve the proper shape. Small pieces and tight curves will require a slightly smaller seam allowance and small stitches close to the edge, in order to avoid tucks and points. Remember that basting means *temporary*, not *big*. When I am basting around a very tight curve or a small circle, I often use a stab stitch and reposition the seam allowance after each up or down stitch, in order to maintain an exact shape.

Basting that is pulled too tightly can draw up the edge of an appliqué piece, causing it to ripple or change shape. Light pressing with the iron, along with clipping a few tight basting stitches, will straighten it out. Take the time to prepare a smooth edge now and the appliqué process will be practically painless!

Once the appliqué pieces have been prepared, they will need to be secured to the background in some way. Most often, I use ½" sequin pins, because they are quick to use and remove, and small enough that they do not catch my thread as I sew. Basting pieces into place is another option.

I find large flat pieces and very fine points easier to do using needle turn. For this approach, the appliqué piece is set into place and the seam allowance is turned under as the stitching progresses around the edge of the appliqué shape. (Fig. 3)

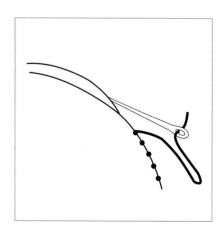

△ *Fig. 3. Needle turn. Point of needle is used to tuck seam allowance under just ahead of appliqué stitches.*

STITCHES

BLINDSTITCH

Most of my appliqué is done using a blindstitch. Done properly, this stitch should live up to its name and not be visible. Begin by choosing a thread that matches the color of the appliqué piece. It is difficult to hide a thread that doesn't match, no matter how good your stitches are.

I begin with a knot, put behind the background block. Trim any long tails from your thread, so that they don't shadow through later. As the needle comes up from behind, it should catch just the very edge of the appliqué piece. To make the next stitch, take the needle down through the background only, right beside the stitch which just came up.

Advance along the underneath surface and come up again, piercing the edge of the appliqué piece as before. (Fig. 4) The thread does not advance on the top, but simply wraps over the edge of the patch. If pulled with the proper tension, the thread should drop down into the weave of the appliqué fabric and be hidden. Appliqué stitches should be small, tight, and close together, to hold the piece firmly in place, but not so tight as to cause distortion.

RUNNING STITCH

Once in a while, I like to use a running stitch along the edge of an appliqué piece. It is done in much the same way as the quilting stitch, working up and down along the folded edge. (Fig. 5) A running stitch can be done with pre-basted edges or while needle turning. The up and down line of the running stitch gives a slightly textured effect to the edges of the appliqué piece. I have used it to appliqué bows and find that it gives them the look of grosgrain ribbon. A matching thread will add texture only, while a contrasting thread will add an additional decorative touch. Running stitch appliqué is not as durable as a close blindstitch, and should probably be reserved for show pieces.

BUTTONHOLE STITCH

Another visible stitch sometimes used for appliqué is the buttonhole stitch. This stitch was used in nineteenth-century chintz work and showed up again in 1930's and 1940's appliqué. It is also a great stitch to use for a folk art look. Refer to the embroidery section of the book for further discussion of this stitch.

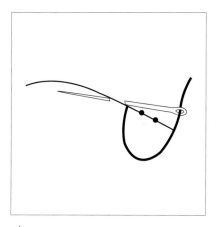

△ *Fig. 4. Blindstitch. Stitch comes up through folded edge. Stitch goes down into background directly beside where it comes up. Needle works parallel to edge of appliqué. Thread advances behind background block.*

△ *Fig. 5. Running Stitch. Up and down stitch through folded edge.*

DIMENSIONAL APPLIQUÉ

Dimension and detail can be added to a quilt in many ways. Some elements need only the illusion of dimension. Layering of appliqué pieces will automatically bring some pieces forward and add depth to a design. Leaves that fold over on themselves or ribbons that twist and turn will appear to have dimension. The effect of light and shadow can be achieved by using fabrics with subtle value changes, or by blending colors for embroidery work.

Cording, padding, and stuffing can be used to create raised areas in appliqué. Bringing appliqué shapes up from the surface of the quilt adds not only visual texture, but also true dimension to the piece.

Ruching can be used to create a gathered or wrinkled surface texture within an appliqué piece. Ruched strips can also be shaped into flowers and other embellishments which stand free from the quilt surface.

Folding, pleating, rolling, facing, and other free-form techniques will produce three-dimensional elements, enabling you to create pieces that seem very real.

Dimensional techniques can be incorporated into any appliqué work. Working with traditional patterns, these techniques can be used to recreate beautiful album quilts in the most elaborate mid-nineteenth-century style. Texture and dimension can also be adapted to create pieces which are very innovative in design. I have enjoyed combining these techniques with my own appliqué designs to develop a style that maintains its traditional roots, but at the same time has a fresh, new look.

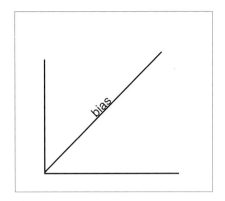

△ *Fig. 6. Usual illustration for bias. Do not cut strips along this line.*

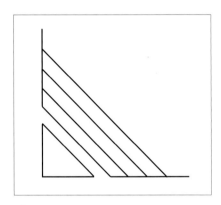

△ *Fig. 7. Cut across corner for bias strips.*

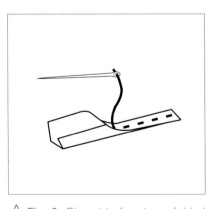

△ *Fig. 8. Bias strip for stems folded lengthwise into thirds and then basted to hold edges in place.*

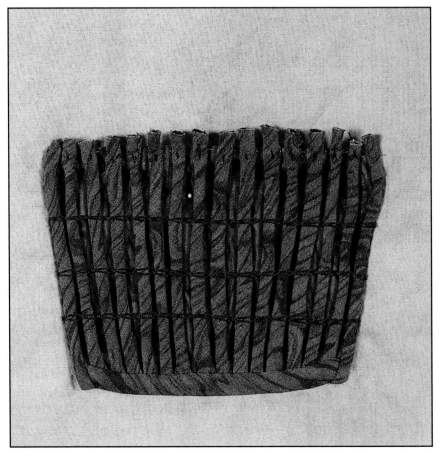

◁ *Bias Strip Example: Twig Basket. Made by Sheila Kennedy.*

◁ *Project #1:* *Flat bias stems.*
Full size pattern on page 98.

BIAS STRIPS

I work with several sizes of stems, from ⅛" (3mm) to ⅓" (8mm) in finished size, depending on the scale of the design. A flower stem is almost always a curved line and should be cut on the bias, so that it can follow the curve and not be distorted.

The quickest and most efficient way to cut bias strips is with a rotary cutter and grid ruler. Although the bias of a fabric is usually shown as running on the diagonal from the corner (Fig. 6), *do not cut your strips along this line.* It is much too wasteful. Cut across the corner, as shown, (Fig. 7) and continue to cut strips parallel to this line to make as many stems as are needed.

To prepare fabric for stems, cut a strip three times as wide as the desired finished size, fold the strip lengthwise into thirds, right side out, and baste to hold the raw edges in place. (Fig. 8) This will give you a stem in its finished size, ready to be put into position on the block. For easier handling, the first fold may be pressed into place with an iron. Press the strip again after it has been basted, to smooth out any gathers caused by the stitching.

I prefer this technique over a sew-and-flip stem because having it free in my hand, but finished in size, allows me to make creative judgments about its placement. I can make last minute changes or even weave stems under and over each other if I like.

Because these tiny bias strips may stretch a little with pressing, or shrink a little as they are sewn down, I generally do not cut them to a finished length until one edge is stitched into place. Be sure to leave enough extra fabric at the end to be covered by the flower. Blindstitch the stem into place, stitching along the concave, or inside curve first, whenever possible, and then along the outside edge.

PROJECT #1: FLAT BIAS STEMS

For the stems in this little block, cut bias strips ½" (13mm) wide and prepare them as directed above. Appliqué the stems in order, beginning with those in the background.

The leaves go on next. They are simple flat appliqué shapes and may be pre-basted or needle-turned. Because the flowers are raised from the surface and may catch threads as you sew, they should be added last. See page 54 for instructions for making the small ruched flowers.

STEM SAMPLER

If you like this method of making stems, you may be interested in making a sampler of different sizes as a reference for future work. I have made a sampler with stems in six different sizes and refer to it often when I am designing. It is helpful to know what width to cut in order to produce a certain finished size.

My smallest stem is cut ⅜" (1 cm) wide. Each one after is ⅛" (3 mm) larger, up to 1" (2.5 cm) wide. It is very surprising to most people that ⅛" (3mm) difference in cut size produces such noticeable results, especially when the strip has been folded into thirds. I use the three smallest measurements most often and cord them all. The larger ones will work well for flat folk art stems or larger scale designs, but may be too heavy looking when corded.

CORDED STEMS

I like to cord stems with yarn for a full natural look. A corded stem is prepared and stitched down in the same way as a flat stem. The cording is put underneath the applied stem as a last step. A bias strip produces the best results for a flat curved stem, and will also stretch easily to accept cording beneath it. Be sure that your appliqué stitches are tight and close together, because the cording will pull the appliqué away from the background just a bit. Do not sew across the ends of the stem.

Polyester rug yarn seems to work best for corded work, as it will compress to squeeze into the tiniest places and then spring back to fill whatever space it occupies. Rug yarn can also be easily split into separate plies for very small stems.

For an average sized stem (cut ½"), thread a blunt tapestry nee-

dle, size 20 or 22, with rug yarn and pull the yarn through the eye to double it. It is not necessary to make a knot in the yarn. Slide the needle and yarn through the channel between the stem and the background block. (Fig. 9) Most often, stem ends will be covered later with a flower or vase and can therefore be left unsewn. The needle can be inserted at one end and pulled out the other with little difficulty.

Leave approximately a ½" (13 mm) tail of yarn at each end of the

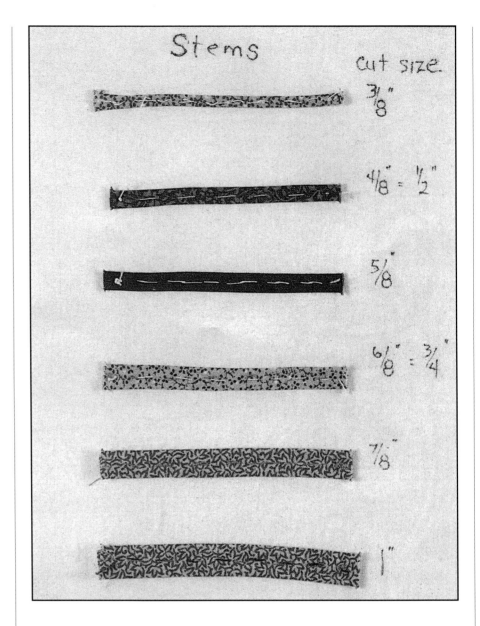

△ *Stem Sampler. Examples are shown finished size. These stems are cut:*
  ⅜" = 1 cm
  ½" = 13 mm
  ⅝" = 16 mm
  ¾" = 19 mm
  ⅞" = 22 mm
  1" = 2.5 cm

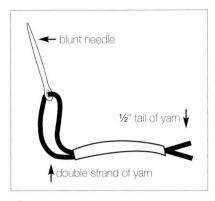

△ *Fig. 9. Corded stem. Stem appliquéd on both sides, ends left open.*

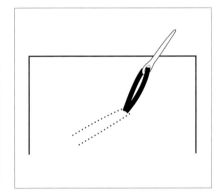

△ *Fig. 10. Stem appliquéd on both sides and one end. Yarn goes in under open end and comes out through background block behind closed stem end.*

▷ *Project #2: Cherry Stem, corded stem. Full size pattern on page 99.*

stem, spreading it out a little to ease the transition from the raised stem to the piece which will cover it.

When I have trouble pulling yarn through a tight space, I use a tool with locking handles to hold onto the needle (a hemostat in medical terms). These "grippers" are beginning to show up in shops and catalogs, and are very handy.

PROJECT #2: CHERRY STEM

Any of the stems presented in this book can be corded. This cherry stem will allow you to try a small sample. Cut a strip ½" (13 mm) wide by 2" (5 cm) long and follow the previous directions for appliquéing and cording. See page 22 for padded cherries.

When leaves, stems, or other motifs are appliquéd on top of a corded stem, it is not necessary to stitch completely through to the background block. Stitch the edge of the appliqué to the surface of the stem. This will allow you to take smaller stitches and will not distort the shape of the stem as deeper stitches might.

If the design dictates that the stem be closed at one end, it can still be corded. Appliqué the stem into place by sewing along one side, turning the end under and stitching it closed, and sewing along the other side to finish. Slide the needle and yarn in under the open end, along the stem, and then exit by piercing the back of the block behind the closed stem end. (Fig. 10) Trim the end of the yarn closely at the closed end, so that no tail remains to make a lump or to shadow through the background.

PROJECT #3: PUSSY WILLOW

These pussy willow branches are made of bias strips cut ⅝" (1.6 cm) wide, folded into thirds, and appliquéd with the tops sewn closed. Taper the tops of the branches slightly for a more realistic look. Cord the branches with a double strand of rug yarn, taking the needle in under the open end at the bottom and out through the background behind the top.

Stems with a tight curve may also require penetrating the background block in order to change the direction of the needle. To continue, come back in through the same hole and pull the yarn back into the channel, so that none remains to create a lump on the back. Draw the yarn carefully through the channel, so that it does not distort the background block. Repeat until the entire length is filled. If the yarn fills the space completely, it will not shift and there is no need to secure it further.

FREE CORDED STEMS

Occasionally, I want a corded stem to weave over and under another stem. I can get this effect by creating a finished free-form stem and then cording it before it is applied.

Begin with a bias strip, folded in half lengthwise, right sides together. Stitch the long raw edges together and turn the strip right side out. The stitching may be done by hand or machine. Turning such a narrow strip is the trick!

The best tool that I have used for this is the Fasturn®. The stitched fabric strip is placed over the outside of a long metal tube. A small wire is used to catch one end of the fabric and pull it through the tube and right side out. The size 2 will work for most stems. You can also sew the fabric tube over a length of yarn or cord and use it to pull the tube right side out, or a small safety pin fastened at one end can be run through the tube and out the other

◁ *Project #3: Pussy Willow, corded stem, closed end. Full size pattern on page 100.*

▽ *Project #4: Grape stem, free corded stem. Full size pattern on page 101.*

end. After the stem has been turned, fill it with a double strand of rug yarn.

PROJECT #4: GRAPE STEM

Cut a bias strip ¾" (19 mm) wide and approximately 5" (12.7 cm) long. Fold the strip in half, right sides together and sew a ³⁄₁₆" (.5 cm) seam. Turn the finished stem right side out and fill it, using a blunt needle and a double strand of rug yarn. Prepare the shorter leaf stem and finish it in the same manner as the cherry stem in Project #2.

With a pin or a basting stitch, secure one end of the free stem in place beneath the main vine. The other end will be positioned later.

Prepare the main vine as directed on the pattern page and appliqué into place across the ends of the leaf and grape stems. Stitch along the lower edge of this vine first, even though it is the convex edge. Be sure that you have covered and secured the two smaller stem ends before you appliqué the top edge of the main vine into place. Cord this vine with two strands of yarn.

Pull the free end of the grape stem up over the vine and into position for the grapes. These free stems have a lovely dimensional look and may be left free, or attached more securely on a piece that will be used.

PADDED APPLIQUÉ

Some shapes, such as fruit or animals, can benefit from a layer of padding underneath. It gives them a smooth rounded shape and makes them seem more real. This work is all done from the top, and does not require cutting through the back of the block.

I prefer to use cotton or one of the new poly/cotton blend battings for my padded work. It is important that the layer of padding is sturdy enough to hold its shape and not shrink later if the quilt is washed. Cotton and blend battings are easy to handle and cut with a clean edge. These raised areas are more likely to receive abrasion, so it is important to use a batt that will not beard.

Fairfield Cotton Classic®, Hobbs Heirloom Cotton®, and Mountain Mist Blue Ribbon® cotton batts all work well. Cotton Classic and Hobbs Heirloom Cotton are very stable batts. Cotton Classic has the lowest loft of the three, but can be used double if desired. Cotton Classic and Blue Ribbon can be split in half for a very thin layer. Read and follow the manufacturer's directions for pre-shrinking if necessary.

PROJECT #5: PADDED CHERRIES

All of the cherries in this block are made from the same template. A layer or two of batting underneath will give them good shape.

Only one template is needed for the appliqué piece and its padding. Add seam allowance as you cut out each cherry from the fabric. Baste the edges under. Place the pre-basted shapes onto a single or double layer of batting and cut an exact shape to fit underneath each one. Position the appliqué piece, with its padding underneath, on the background block. Simply appliqué the piece into place, as usual, tucking in the edges of the batting as you stitch.

If you have padded an area and find that it is not full enough to suit you, it is possible to add more padding without removing the entire appliqué and starting over. For a small piece like these cherries, you can cut a slit in the background and slip in another layer of batting from behind. Use a toothpick or a long pin to smooth out the edges. A larger piece can be done in the same way, or shape may be added in the form of loose stuffing put in behind the layer of padding. Do not cut away the backing fabric, as it is needed to hold the padding in place.

A layer of batting also works well to prevent seam allowances or other fabric pieces from shadowing through, which can be a real problem when you are layering light appliqué pieces over dark.

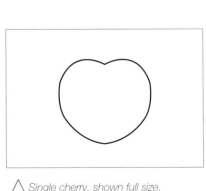

△ *Single cherry, shown full size.*

◁ *Project #5: Padded Cherries. Full size pattern on page 99.*

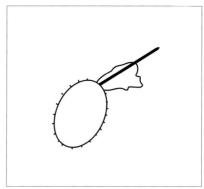

△ *Fig. 11. Stuffed grapes. Appliqué grape flat, and just before the last two or three stitiches are taken, insert stuffing with a wooden toothpick.*

◁ *Project #6: Grapes. Full size pattern on page 101.*

STUFFED APPLIQUÉ

Some appliqué pieces may be stuffed rather than padded. Grapes and flower centers are good examples. Adding loose stuffing between the layers is easier than cutting to size many tiny shapes for padding.

As with the padded work, I prefer to use a cotton or blend batting for stuffing. It can be pulled into tiny wisps and inserted a little at a time with a wooden toothpick. Cotton gives a good dense filling and does not have the unruly fibers of polyester.

Insert enough stuffing to give a full natural shape, but not so much that it strains the edges of the piece. When the motif is as full as desired, take the final stitches to finish the appliqué. If you find that the piece has a lumpy surface after it is stuffed, it is possible to rearrange the stuffing with a long straight pin worked through the top or back of the piece. Take care not to snag or tear the fabric.

STUFFING FROM THE SURFACE
PROJECT #6: GRAPES

The grapes in this block are all made from a single template. Mark and cut them out, adding seam allowance. It is probably easiest to judge placement of so many pieces in relation to one another if the edges are turned under to allow you to see the finished size. If you are basting, take small stitches, close to the edge in order to keep a smooth shape.

Appliqué the grapes into place, using small, close, tight blindstitches, just as for flat appliqué. Try to catch just the very edge of the appliqué as you sew. Stitches too deep into the piece will cause the edge to look wrinkled after it is stuffed.

Insert the stuffing just before the last two or three stitches are taken. (Fig. 11) Try to see that all of the grapes are filled equally.

STUFFING MULTIPLE UNITS

This approach to stuffed work can also be used to fill flower petals that have been divided by a line of stitching. Many of the flowers in the Follett House quilt were done in this manner.

The flower shape is drawn onto one flat piece of fabric, with lines to mark the petal divisions. Before the outside edge is appliquéd down, a line of stitching is used to divide the flower into sections and secure it to the background block. Each section is stuffed as the grapes were done, and then the edges are sewn closed. (Fig. 12)

PROJECT #7: FOLLETT HOUSE FLOWER

Draw the flower as shown, including the outline and all of the petal details, onto the right side of a single piece of fabric.

Position the flower on the block, over the finished stem, and secure it with tiny pins. For this project, use quilting thread to divide the petal sections and to secure the flower to the background. You will be quilting together only the two layers of fabric.

Begin by quilting around the flower center, stopping just two or three stitches short of closing the circle. Place stuffing between the layers to fill the center and then finish the quilting line to hold the stuffing in place.

Quilt a line between each petal, from the center to the seam allowance line at the outer edge of the flower.

Clip the seam allowance between each petal, stopping just short of the line of quilting.

One at a time, stuff each petal and needle turn the edge closed. Use sewing weight thread and your best

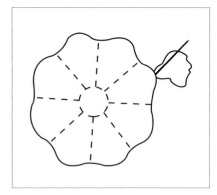

△ *Fig. 12. Follett House Flower. Quilted lines separate sections. Stuff between layers. Appliqué outside edges last.*

▷ *Project #8: Stuffed Buds. Full size pattern on page 103.*

▽ *Project #7: Follett House Flower. Full size pattern on page 102.*

blindstitch here as with any other appliqué. Be careful to maintain the outside shape of the petals as you work.

If you are concerned about controlling the outside edges, they may be clipped and basted as a first step, before you begin to quilt the layers together.

Various stitches and types of thread can be used to separate the petals for flowers worked in this way. The Follett House quilt includes flowers stitched with sewing thread and crewel wool, in matching and contrasting colors, in outline stitch and running stitch! Think about the look you want and work to achieve it.

STUFFING BETWEEN LAYERS

Stuffing from the surface is particularly useful when working with layered appliqué. The top motif can be stuffed without cutting through several layers of appliqué beneath it.

PROJECT #8: STUFFED BUDS

These stuffed buds are from the Follett House quilt and have a more traditional and slightly primitive look. Cut the calyx in a full triangular shape. It is not necessary to cut out the "v" shape that lies behind the bud. Appliqué the bud on top of the calyx shape and stuff it just before finishing the appliqué stitches.

The rose hairs at the top of these buds were worked with silk twist in the original quilt. I used a sewing weight thread and worked fine lines of stem stitches. They could also be inked.

STUFFING FROM BEHIND

If a flower has petal divisions that are not open to the outside edge, stuffing can be added by working through the background block. In this case, the outside edges are appliquéd down first, either pre-basted or by needle turn, and the sections are divided by a line of stitching. The stuffing is added last, through a slit in the background fabric.

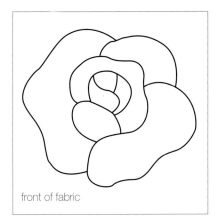

front of fabric

△ *Fig. 13. Stuffed Appliqué Rose (stuffed from behind). Draw rose as shown on single piece of fabric. Appliqué into place. Embroider all inside lines. Full size pattern on page 104.*

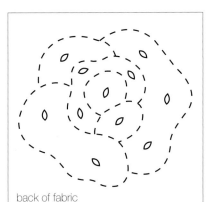

back of fabric

△ *Fig. 14. Back of Stuffed Appliqué Rose. Turn block over and cut slit behind each section. Stuff. Embroider outside edge.*

▷ *Project #9: Stuffed Appliqué Rose (stuffed from behind). Full size pattern on page 104.*

PROJECT #9: ROSE

Mark the flower as before, on a single piece of fabric (Fig. 13) and appliqué it into place, using a blind-stitch around the outside edge. For this project, all of the petal divisions are added with an embroidery line worked through the flower and background block. Again, there are many options as to type of thread, color, and stitch. I used a double ply of embroidery floss in a matching color, worked in a stem stitch, for a rich textured line. I left the center of my rose to be stuffed as one piece and then embroidered the "Y" details onto the surface after it was stuffed. See page 73 for stem stitch embroidery.

When the embroidery is finished, turn the block over and carefully cut a tiny slit in the background fabric behind each of the petal sections. (Fig. 14) A small pair of scissors with very sharp points works well to catch and lift the backing fabric away from the flower. Take care that you do not cut through the layer of appliqué fabric. Stuff the petals as full as you like, keeping them smooth and even. Embroider around the outside edge of the rose, using the same thread and stitch, to finish it.

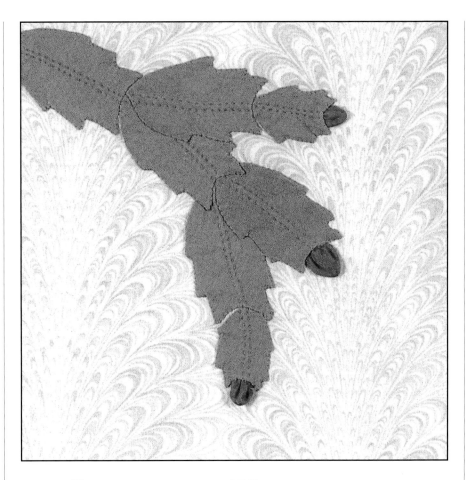

CHANNEL TRAPUNTO

The term trapunto originally was used to identify raised work produced by running cord through a quilted channel in whole cloth. Cording can also be put into a quilted channel to produce a raised line within an appliqué piece.

PROJECT #10: CHRISTMAS CACTUS

Begin by appliquéing the motif to the block. The Christmas cactus is made in separate sections and appliquéd with one piece overlapping the next. The buds should be made and inserted into the ends of the cactus as it is being appliquéd. They must be in place before the channels are begun. See page 44 for gathered buds.

When the appliqué is finished, stitch two parallel lines to create a channel along the center line of each section. Use a running stitch to hold the two layers of fabric together. (Fig. 15) The thread used for this should be a matching color and can be a sewing weight thread. There will be no strain on the stitches once the yarn is in place. The width of the channel should be approximately ⅛" (3 mm), but will vary with the scale of the design.

Once the channel is in place, work from the back of the block and use a tapestry needle and yarn to fill the channel in the same manner as for the corded stem. (Fig. 16) For these narrow channels, divide a length of rug yarn into separate plies. Thread one ply through a blunt needle and pull to double it. This double ply will give you the correct thickness for the project.

◁ *Project #10: Christmas Cactus. Full size pattern on page 105.*

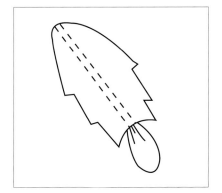

△ *Fig. 15. Channel trapunto. Two parallel lines of running stitches ⅛" apart form the channel, stitched through appliqué and background block.*

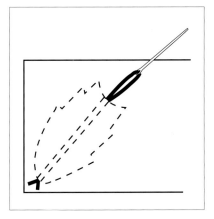

△ *Fig. 16. Turn block over and pull yarn through channel, going in and out by piercing background block. Trim yarn ends closely.*

△ *Fig. 17. Reverse Appliqué. Cut center out. Window template full size on page 106.*

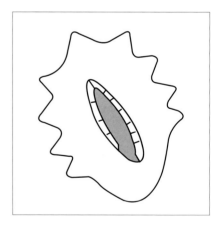

△ *Fig. 18. Reverse Appliqué. Seam allowance clipped. Contrasting fabric underneath if desired. Appliqué outside edges first. Needle turn inside edges.*

◁ *Project #11: Reverse Appliqué – Traditional Stylized Flower. Full size pattern on page 106.*

▷ *Project #12: Padded Reverse Appliqué – Stylized Bud. Full size pattern on page 107.*

REVERSE APPLIQUÉ

I use reverse appliqué as an accent, for small details or areas of color within an appliqué piece, and when areas need to be recessed to give a natural appearance or to prevent a build up of many layers. With the reverse appliqué technique you can plan to have the background fabric show through the cutout area, or add another color behind the appliqué.

TRADITIONAL
PROJECT #11: STYLIZED FLOWER

This folk art flower has a reverse appliquéd center with an accent color showing through.

A window template seems to be the simplest way to approach this type of work. To make your template, draw the design onto plastic or paper, whichever you prefer. Cut around the outside shape and then cut out along the center markings as well, to create a window. (Fig. 17)

Place the template onto the appliqué fabric and mark both the outside and inside lines. If the lengthwise line of the cut out area is positioned on the bias, the seam allowances will have a little stretch and will be much easier to turn.

When you cut the fabric, be sure that you add seam allowance around the outside, and also inside the lines marked for the center detail. If you cut along the marked lines, you will have nothing to turn under. The center seam allowance will need to be clipped into the points and a few times along the curved edges for ease in turning. Clip between each point along the outside edge as well.

If you want an accent color to show through the cutout, cut this fabric larger than the opening. If the under fabric has pattern, use the window template to plan what will show through.

Layer this fabric under the top flower piece and pin or baste the pieces securely to the background block. (Fig. 18) Appliqué the outside edges first. This will stabilize the flower and make it easier to needle

turn the center.

Before stitching the center opening, check to see that the underneath fabric is positioned correctly. Stitch through all three layers to hold everything in place.

PADDED REVERSE APPLIQUÉ

Sometimes a motif which will look best done in reverse appliqué will also seem to require padding. I have found that working the reverse appliqué onto a layer of batting before it is appliquéd to the block allows me to combine both of these techniques.

PROJECT #12: STYLIZED BUD

Again, use a window template to

mark and cut the calyx and underlying bud fabrics. For the green calyx, which will lie on top of the flower color, position the template on the right side of the fabric. Mark around the outside edge and also mark inside the window for the area that will be cut out. Add seam allowance both inside and out.

Because this bud is so small, use the same template to mark and cut the underneath flower fabric the same size. (Fig. 19, page 30) It is not necessary to add seam allowance to this piece because its edges will be covered by the calyx. Do not mark or cut out the center of this piece, or you will have nothing to show through!

Baste around the outside edges

of the calyx to turn the seam allowance under. (Fig. 20) It is easier to take care of this step now rather than after the piece has been placed on the batting. Clip the curved edges and the point of the cut-out area in the center. Position the calyx over the flower fabric and then pin both to a layer of batting. (Fig. 21) Use a piece of batting that will be a comfortable size to handle. It will be trimmed to size later.

Work the reverse appliqué center, stitching completely through the batt. I find this center area easiest to appliqué by needle turning. Be sure to use a thread that matches the green calyx and not the flower center. *Do not appliqué the outside edge.*

When the center is finished, trim away the batting and any of the flower fabric that might be showing along the outside edge. (Fig. 22) Position the finished bud as you like. Appliqué with a blindstitch, tucking in the batting if necessary, so that you are sewing through the edge of the appliqué fabric only.

▷ *Fig. 19.* (Left) Padded Reverse Appliqué – Stylized Bud.
Flower fabric, no seam allowance.

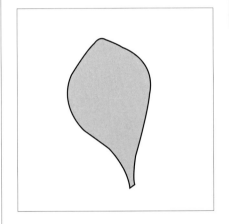

▷ *Fig. 20.* (Right) Padded Reverse Appliqué – Stylized Bud.
Calyx with outer edges basted under and inner seam allowance clipped.

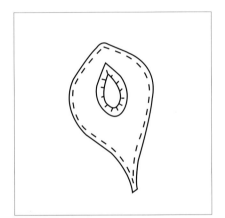

▷ *Fig. 21.* (Left) Padded Reverse Appliqué – Stylized Bud.
Fabrics layered on small piece of batting.

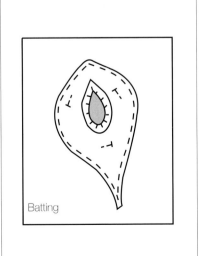

▷ *Fig. 22.* (Right) Padded Reverse Appliqué – Stylized Bud.
Needle turn center in, reverse appliqué. Trim away excess batting.

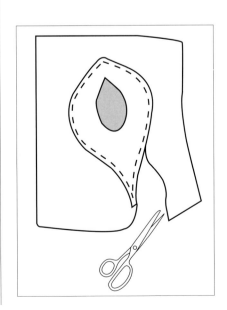

◁ *Project #13: Morning Glory.*
Full size pattern on page 108.

SURFACE STITCHING ON PADDED APPLIQUÉ

A layer of padding beneath appliqué adds body to the piece and raises it up from the background block. This creates a kind of mini-quilt which can be stitched or embellished to add even more surface texture.

EMBROIDERY:

Rather than cutting separate petals for some flowers, a line of embroidery can be worked through a padded appliqué to define the petal shapes.

PROJECT #13: MORNING GLORY

Mark the outline and petal details of the morning glory blossom onto a single piece of fabric. Baste the outside edge and appliqué the flower over a layer of batting, as you did with the padded cherries (Project #5).

When the appliqué is finished, use a single ply of thread or floss and work a line of stem stitches to divide the petals. Embroidering through all of the layers will add a little dimension to the flower.

QUILTING:

A padded motif can also be quilted to add texture and visual interest. There are several benefits to quilting a padded appliqué at this stage. It is much easier to quilt this area now, before more layers are added. The thread that is used can be any color and will not show on the back of the quilt. When the whole quilt is layered and the surrounding areas are quilted, the motif will have texture and still stand away from the background.

PROJECT #14: HEART LOCKET

Appliqué this framed heart using the padded reverse appliqué technique (Project #12, page 29). Quilt along the inside edge of the frame and then add whatever quilting pattern you like to the center of the heart.

▷ *Project #14:* Heart Locket.
Full size pattern on page 109.

UNIT APPLIQUÉ

A motif which is made of many pieces is sometimes easier to apply if the sections are joined first. This idea is also very useful when working with a motif that appears to fold over on itself, such as a folded leaf or ribbon. It will help to eliminate the bulk at those very fine points.

Unit appliqués can be padded or stuffed without cutting a separate piece of batting to be layered under each part. By joining the pieces of the appliqué to create the entire motif separate from the background, the layer of padding can be added all at one time.

Unit appliqués can be further embellished before they are sewn to the background. It is often easier to do detail work on this smaller piece, rather than working through many layers later.

FINE POINTS

PROJECT #15: FOLDED LEAVES

Leaves that fold over on themselves can give a natural look to a bouquet or flower arrangement. A problem can arise, though, when one section of the leaf seems to disappear into a very fine point. (Fig. 23) It is difficult to hide all of the seam allowance under this point without making a lump. But by joining the sections before turning the seam allowances, you can do it perfectly.

△ *Fig. 23.* Folded Leaf.

◁ *Project #15: Violets – Folded Leaves. Full size pattern on page 110.*

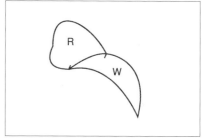

△ *Fig. 24. Hash marks on templates. Draw template as one piece. Mark right and wrong sides. Put hash marks where templates join.*

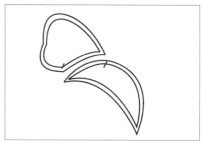

△ *Fig. 25. Cut templates apart and draw shapes onto fabric. Hash marks extend into seam allowance of fabric.*

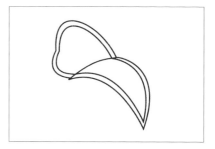

△ *Fig. 26. Overlap and sew pieces together from mark to mark.*

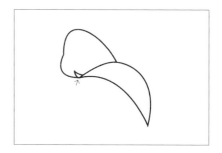

△ *Fig. 27. Seam allowance around point falls beneath adjacent piece.*

Draw your templates for the leaf as one unit, rather than separate parts. Decide which part of the leaf is the "right" side and which is the "wrong" side, and mark this information on the templates. Before cutting the templates apart, put hash marks on each piece to show where they overlap. (Fig. 24)

Folded leaves can be made using the same fabric for both pieces, the right and wrong sides of a print fabric, or two different fabrics.

For the part of the leaf that is the "right" side, place this template right side up on the chosen fabric and draw a line around it. For the "wrong" side, place this template right side up on the fabric chosen for this section and draw around it. Transfer the hash marks from the templates out into the seam allowances of each piece. (Fig. 25) These marks will be used to align the pieces when they are joined.

Decide which piece of the leaf comes forward or closer to the viewer. Looking only at the seam allowance where the two pieces overlap, finger press under the seam allowance of this forward piece and place it on top of the other. Use the hash marks to insure proper alignment. With a blind appliqué stitch sew from marked edge to marked edge, leaving the outside seam allowances free. (Fig. 26)

After the pieces have been joined, turn under the seam allowance around the entire leaf. You will see that the bulk of the seam allowance around the fine point will automatically fall beneath the adjacent piece for a perfectly smooth edge. (Fig. 27)

▷ *Project #16: Ribbons and Bows. Full size pattern on page 111.*

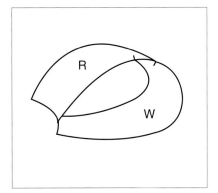

△ *Fig. 28. Templates drawn as one unit. Mark right and wrong sides. Hash marks indicate where pieces join.*

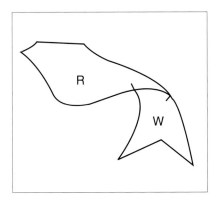

△ *Fig. 29. Hash marks on templates.*

PROJECT #16: RIBBONS AND BOWS

When appliquéd ribbons appear to twist and turn over on themselves, they often leave us with very fine points to execute. (Fig. 28) This problem can be solved by handling the whole bow loop or streamer as one unit, as with the folded leaves.

When making your templates, draw each bow loop or streamer as one piece. It may have three or more parts, but do not draw them as individual templates. As the ribbon turns over, it shows us, alternately, its right and wrong sides. Decide which pieces are "right" sides and which are "wrong" and mark the templates as such. Add hash marks at the places where the templates join, so that the fabric pieces will also join each other properly to create the desired flow. (Fig. 29)

I enjoy making ribbons with fabrics that have a good solid color on the reverse side. It gives me the perfect coordinating color and adds to the illusion.

For each piece marked as a "right" side, place the template right side up, on the right side of the fabric and draw a line around it. For each piece marked as a "wrong" side, place the template right side up, on the wrong side of the fabric and draw around it. Transfer the hash marks from the templates out into the seam allowances of each fabric piece. (Fig. 30) It is important for the visual flow of the ribbon that outlines and joining seams be extremely accurate. Do not try to join these pieces or turn the edges "by eye".

Take two pieces that are to be

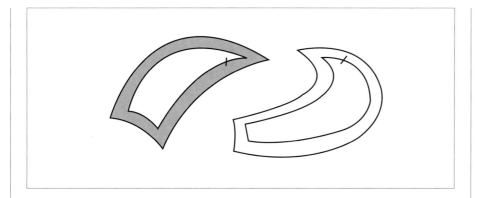

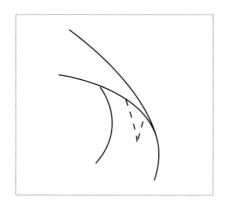

◁ *Fig. 30. Cut templates apart. Mark on right and wrong sides of fabric. Extend hash marks into seam allowance of fabric.*

◁ *Fig. 31. Join adjacent pieces. Do not sew through seam allowance.*

◁ *Fig. 32. Turn seam allowance under around entire unit. Bulk from fine points falls beneath adjacent piece.*

joined. Study the pattern for the flow of the ribbon and decide which part of the ribbon is on top as it folds over. Finger press the seam allowance of this piece under, between the hash marks, where it will be joined to the next piece. Place this piece on top of the adjacent piece, using the hash marks to assure proper placement.

Working from the right side so that you can see your work, blindstitch one piece to the other. Stitch only the area where the two pieces are joined, leaving the seam allowance unsewn. (Fig. 31) Take care to see that the pieces line up properly and that seams which curve are not flattened out. You may need to clip a little on a concave curve, just as with any other appliqué piece. Attach all of the pieces needed to form a complete bow loop or streamer.

Now you are ready to turn under the seam allowance around this whole unit. Clip any other curve that might need it. You will see that when the edges are turned under on these units, the seam allowance around the fine points naturally falls under the piece beyond it and creates no bulk at all. (Fig. 32)

Pre-basting the seam allowance on these ribbons will show you the finished look before it is sewn down. The ribbons can also be appliquéd into place by needle turning the edges. Take care to follow the drawn outlines carefully and to ease the joining seams into place.

For a little added texture, I have found that appliquéing with a running stitch in a matching color thread gives the edges of the ribbon a grosgrain

appearance.

PADDED UNIT APPLIQUÉ

A motif with only a few simple pieces may be pieced, or overlapped and appliquéd together, then padded as the cherries were in Project #5. However, some motifs will have very tiny pieces which may be difficult to handle. I have found that working each piece directly onto a base layer of batting makes the project more manageable.

Because I make most of my final design decisions in fabric rather than on paper, I have found another advantage in creating pieces which are "finished" but free from the background. I can see exactly how the motif fits into the whole design and can make last minute decisions about its placement.

PROJECT #17: CHICKADEE

Mark and cut pieces for the chickadee as for any other appliqué. Baste under the seam allowances on each edge that will show on the finished piece. Edges that will be covered by another piece need not be turned. Assemble the pieces in their proper places on a single layer of batting. Use a matching thread to appliqué along each edge which overlaps another. *Do not appliqué any outside edges*. Take stitches completely through the layer of batting. When the pieces have been joined, trim away the excess batting, leaving just enough to pad the piece. You will find that stitching through the batting has added slight texture to the motif. This texture will not be lost when the piece is appliquéd into place on the block.

STRIP PIECING

Occasionally an appliqué motif can be designed to take advantage of strip piecing. When I looked at pussy willow buds and their cases, I found a good use for this time-saving technique.

▽ *Project #17: Chickadee. Full size pattern on page 112.*

△ *Project #18: Pussy Willow.*
Full size pattern on page 100.

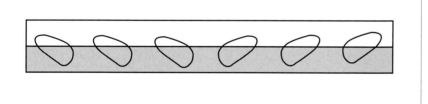

◁ *Fig. 33. Mark and cut the pussy willow and its cap at the same time.*

PROJECT #18: PUSSY WILLOW

Cut one light and one dark strip of fabric, on grain, ¾" x 12" (1.9 cm x 30 cm). Piece the strips together, using ⅛" (3 mm) seam. Press the seam allowance toward the dark fabric to prevent shadow through and also to give a raised edge to the darker fabric which will be the pussy willow cap. Lay the template across the seam, as shown in figure 33, to mark and cut the pussy willow and its cap at the same time. Cut five or six in each direction.

Position the blossoms along the stems in a pleasing arrangement. Appliqué and stuff each one as you did with the grapes in Project #6. Be sure to use matching thread to appliqué the light and dark sections of each pussy willow blossom.

EMBELLISHED UNIT APPLIQUÉ
PROJECT #19: DAISY

A multi-petaled flower with perspective will require a different template for each petal. Keeping track of so many templates, properly positioning the petals, and fitting the center can be a challenge. Perhaps you want to further embellish the center by stuffing or embroidering it, but do not want to work through the background layers. Creating the flower as a free unit on a piece of batting can solve all of these problems.

The center of this type of flower can be made from a fabric with good visual texture or can be embroidered for real texture. If the center is to be embroidered with knots, mark around the template onto the desired fabric, but do not cut it out. Place the piece of fabric into a small hoop and work the embroidery. Refer to the embroidery section, if necessary, for French or Colonial knots. When the embroidery is finished, cut around the shape, leaving a generous seam allowance.

Draw the complete flower, as shown, onto freezer paper or another heavy paper to use as "disposable" templates. Do not draw them as separate petals or number the templates in order to try to use them again. I find that I can trace another flower more quickly than I can sort and position this many little template pieces.

Begin with any petal. Cut a single paper petal away from the drawn flower and position it on your fabric. Mark around the template and cut out the petal adding a narrow seam allowance. Baste the seam allowance under and pin this petal into place on a layer of Fairfield's Cotton Classic® or Hobbs Thermore® batting. Go back to the paper template, cut the next petal and repeat the process. Take the petals in order until you have worked your way around the entire flower and all of the petals have been basted and are pinned in their correct position on the batting. (Fig. 34)

Place the prepared center onto the petals to check the fit. (Fig. 35) At this point, the petals are still free and can be adjusted to make sure that the center covers the end of each one. If it does not, reposition the petals until

they are right. Snip the knots from the basting thread in each petal before sewing the center into place. Appliqué around the center, making sure to stitch through the end of each petal and through the layer of batting.

The flower center can be stuffed at this point, without having to cut through the background block, leaves, stems, or whatever else might be in the way if the flower were in place on the block. Turn the flower over and carefully cut a slit in the batting behind the flower center. (Fig. 36)

Trim little wisps of batting and use them to stuff the flower center nice and full.

Trim the batting around the petals, leaving just enough to pad each one. (Fig. 37) The flower is now complete and ready to appliqué into place. Because it is completely finished and free from the background, you can position it as you like. The padding adds dimension and also assures that you will have no shadow showing through, which is especially important with white daisy petals.

▽ *Project #19: Daisy.*
Full size pattern on page 113.

Batting

△ *Fig. 34 Baste under seam allowance on each petal. Pin in place.*

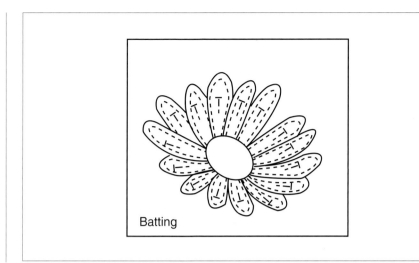

Batting

△ *Fig. 35. Check fit of center. Sew center in place.*

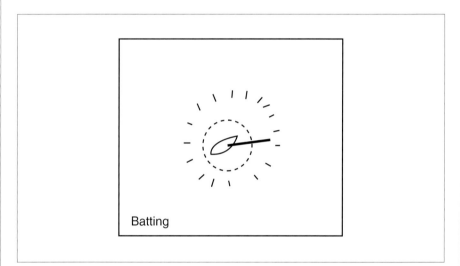

Batting

◁ *Fig. 36. Turn to wrong side. Cut slit behind center and stuff it full.*

◁ *Fig. 37. Trim away excess batting.*

FREE-FORM APPLIQUÉ

FACED

Free-form flower petals or leaves can be made by facing them with another piece of fabric. Prepare your template and fabric as usual for the top side of the piece.

Decide on fabric for the underside. It could be the same as the top fabric, the reverse of the fabric, or a different fabric altogether. Reverse the template to mark this piece.

A thin layer of batting between the layers will give the motif some body. I prefer to use a half layer of Fairfield's Cotton Classic® or Hobbs Thermore® batting. This technique works best on shapes with smooth outlines and gentle curves.

PROJECT #20: OAK LEAVES

Layer the two fabric pieces, right sides together, and put the batting piece against the top fabric. Machine stitch around the outside edges. If the design is such that the stem end of the leaf will be covered by other appliqué, leave this area open. If the leaf hangs completely free, as this one does, sew the entire edge closed.

Clip all of the inner curves in the seam allowance. Trim most of the batting away from the seam to eliminate bulk. If the leaf has been left unsewn at the top, turn it right side out through this opening. If it has been sewn closed, split the underside along the center vein line and turn the shape

right side out. Be sure that the outside edges are pushed out to their full and proper shape. If the underside has been cut, whipstitch these edges together. Press the leaf lightly to make it lie flat. Use a running stitch or stem stitch to secure the finished leaf to the block along the vein lines, leaving the edges free.

FUSED FABRIC

Two layers of fabric can also be fused together to create free-form petals and leaves. Since this technique does not require the pieces to be stitched and turned, it can be used to create shapes with very sharp points. Use one of the fabric bonding sheets made for fusing shapes in place for machine appliqué.

PROJECT #21: FUCHSIA PETALS

Cut two pieces of fabric, approximately 2" x 2" (5 cm x 5 cm) and fuse them together, right sides out. Follow the fusing instructions on the product you are using. Let the piece cool a minute or two. Mark and cut the pointed upper petals from this fused fabric. The edges need no further finishing. Baste the petals into place over the stuffed cap of the flower.

FOLDED
PROJECT #22: FOLDED BUDS

Folded buds begin with a circle, folded in half. (Fig. 38) Fold the half circle into thirds and baste along the raw edge to hold the folds in place. (Fig. 39) Position the bud under the calyx. As you appliqué the calyx into place, stitch through the base of the bud to the background block. It might be necessary to use a stab stitch to sew through all of the layers.

Variation: Gather along the bottom edge to draw this up into a slightly rounded shape.

◁ *Project #20:* *Oak Leaves.*
Full size pattern on page 114.

▷ *Project #21:* *Fuchsia Petals.*
Full size pattern on page 115.

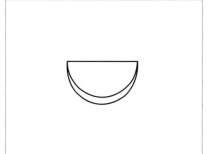

△ *Fig. 38. Fold circle in half.*

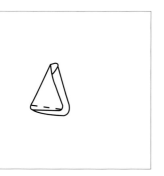

△ *Fig. 39. Fold again into thirds and baste.*

▷ *Project #22:* *Folded Buds.*
Full size pattern on page 116.

PLEATED

Pleated fabric can be used to create a traditional looking dimensional flower.

PROJECT #23: PLEATED FLOWER

Begin with a rectangle of fabric cut on the bias. The stretch of the bias will allow the piece to be shaped more easily.

Press a ¼" (6 mm) hem to the wrong side of the piece along three sides, as shown. (Fig. 40) There is no need to baste. Fold the piece, accordion style, into pleats approximately ⅜" (1 cm) wide. Press the pleats with an iron to hold them in place.

Set the flower in position on the stem. Allow the pleats at the top edge to relax slightly, producing a triangular or fan-shaped flower. (Fig. 41)

Appliqué the flower into place, as usual, along both straight sides. When stitching across the pleated top, appliqué the edges that touch the block, but leave the tips of the forward pleats free. Add the heart-shaped calyx to cover the bottom raw edges. (Fig. 42)

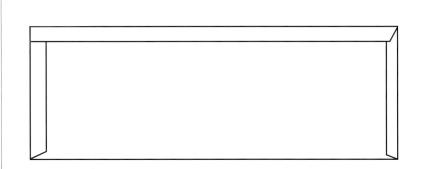

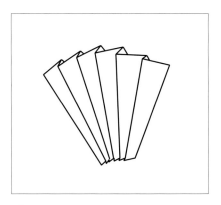

◁ *Fig. 40. Bias rectangle of fabric. Press under ¼" hem along three sides.*

△ *Fig. 41. Fold strip of fabric accordion style. Allow top pleats to relax, producing a fan-shaped flower.*

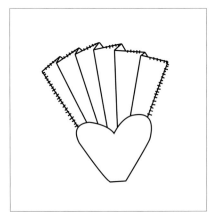

△ *Fig. 42. Blindstitch in place where edges of flower touch background. Add calyx.*

◁ *Project #23: Pleated Flower. Full size pattern on page 117.*

◁ *Project #24: Fuchsia Blossom. Full size pattern on page 115.*

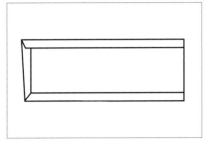

△ *Fig. 43. Turn raw edges in on three sides of strip as shown.*

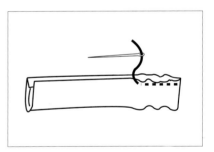

△ *Fig. 44. Turn bottom raw edge up and gather across top.*

△ *Fig. 45. Tuck raw end of strip inside finished end and blindstitch closed.*

RUFFLED

Some flowers, such as fuchsia or columbine, have full ruffled petals which form a part of the flower. This project will produce a ruffled petal which is finished inside and out and gathered across the top.

PROJECT #24: FUCHSIA

Cut a bias strip 1½" x 2½" (3.8 cm x 6.4 cm). Press a narrow hem to the wrong side along three sides, as shown. (Fig. 43) Fold the strip in half, lengthwise, wrong sides together. Using quilting thread, stitch across the top edge and pull to gather. (Fig. 44)

As you approach the opposite end of the strip, tuck the raw edge into the finished edge to form a circle. Finish gathering the top edge and then blind-stitch along the seam to join the ends. (Fig. 45)

The stuffed cap and fused upper petals of the fuchsia must be put in place first. To add the ruffled bottom petals, appliqué the top gathered edge into place, stitching the underneath layer first and then the top layer. Leave the sides and bottom edges free.

Refer to the embroidery section on free threads to add the stamens to this flower.

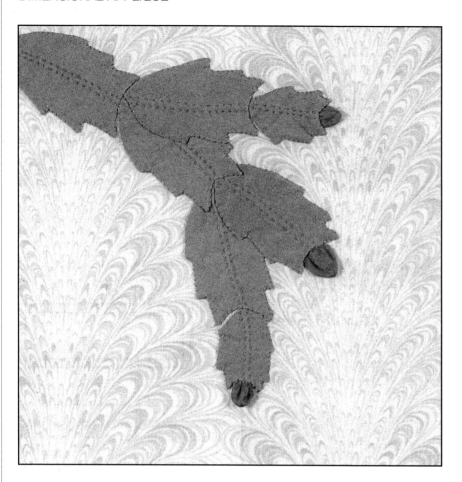

◁ *Project #25:* Christmas Cactus Buds. *Full size pattern on page 105.*

GATHERED

PROJECT #25: GATHERED BUDS

To make tiny gathered flower buds, trace a circle around a small coin or use a circle guide. Cut out the circle on the drawn line and fold it in half. Run a line of stitches along the raw edges (Fig. 46) and pull to draw up the bud to the desired size. (Fig. 47) Secure the bud under the calyx of the flower.

Use these gathered buds in the Christmas cactus block. The smaller bud is 1" (25 mm) or the size of a quarter. Larger buds are 1¼" (3 cm) or the size of a half-dollar.

Variation: this bud can also be rolled after it is gathered, making a more dimensional shape.

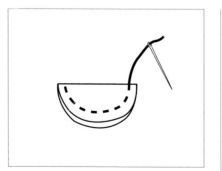

◁ *Fig. 46.* Circle folded in half, gather raw edges.

◁ *Fig. 47.* Pull the line of stitching to draw up the bud.

ROLLED

Flowers such as the iris or morning glory have buds with a rolled shape, which can be reproduced dimensionally.

PROJECT #26: ROLLED BUDS

Cut a rectangular piece of fabric, on grain, and fold it in half lengthwise, right side out. Fold it in half the other direction, but with the edges offset slightly. (Fig. 48) Holding onto the folded corner, wrap and spiral down to form a bud, allowing both folded edges to show. (Fig. 49) Take a stitch or two to secure the end and then wrap the thread around the base to hold it tightly and to help maintain the rolled shape. (Fig. 50) For the morning glory bud, cut a rectangle 1½" x 4" (3.8 cm x 10 cm) and follow the above directions for making a rolled bud.

▽ *Fig. 48 ½" x 4" on grain. Fold in half lengthwise then crosswise (offset).
Folded corner.

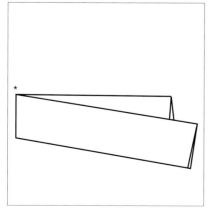

▽ *Fig. 49. Hold onto closed corner. Wrap ends around and spiral down so that both folded edges show.*

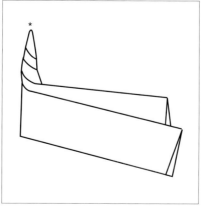

△ *Project #26: Morning Glory Buds. Full size pattern on page 108.*

▽ *Fig. 50. Stitch to hold and then wrap end with thread.*

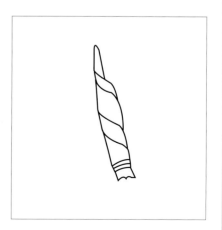

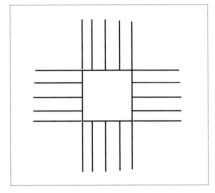

Project #27: Tufts.
Tufts on branch behind satin stitched butterfly. Full size pattern on page 134.

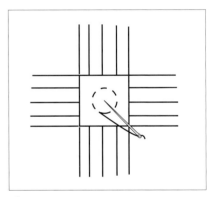

△ *Fig. 51. Square of fabric ½", ¾", or 1" depending on size of flower. Fray out edges, leaving ¼" of fabric in center.*

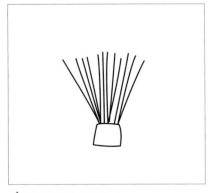

△ *Fig. 52. Stitch small circle in center of fabric. Take stab stitch through center and pull to gather.*

TUFTS OR TORN CENTERS

This little embellishment was suggested by Elly Sienkiewicz. Although these little fuzzies appear to be made from thread, they are actually fabric.

PROJECT #27: TUFTS

Begin by cutting a small square of fabric, ½" to 1" (13 mm to 2.5 cm) in size, depending on the scale of the design. Pull threads along all four edges to make fringe (Fig. 51), leaving a ¼" (6 mm) square of fabric intact in the center. Stitch a tiny circle in the center of the fabric. Then, taking a stab stitch directly through the center (Fig. 52), pull to draw up the fabric, so that only the frayed ends show. (Fig. 53) Use the same thread to stitch it into place. These little tufts work equally well as embellishment on a flat surface, such as the branch behind the satin stitched butterfly (above), or as the center of a ruched flower (Project #38).

△ *Fig. 53. Finished tuft.*

△ *Tufts or Torn Center Sample.* *"Little Bit of Everything," 1990, 24"x 24".*
Designed and made by the author. This basket of flowers was designed for a group in Columbus who wanted to know how to do "everything!" Techniques include corded, padded, and stuffed appliqué, rolled buds, folded leaves, bells, berries, ruched flowers, and unit-appliqué daisies.

BERRIES

Although many antique quilts include berries that are flat or stuffed as the grapes in Project #6, I have seen several quilts from the mid-nineteenth century which have stuffed free-form berries. I love the dimension that these berries add to a design and use them often.

To prepare the fabric for these berries, mark around a circle guide, your thimble, or a coin to make a perfect little circle. I have used a dime for bittersweet, a quarter for most of my berries, and a fifty-cent piece for grapes and blueberries. Experiment with different sizes. You might want to make a berry sampler, as I have done, for reference in future projects.

PROJECT #28: GRAPES

Use a 1¼" circle guide or a fifty-cent piece as a template for these free-form grapes. Cut them out on the drawn line. This size is large enough, without added seam allowance.

Using quilting thread for extra strength and stitching as close to the folded edge as possible, turn under a tiny hem all around your fabric circle. (Fig. 54) Gather it into a cup shape and use a pinch of cotton or blend batting for stuffing. (Fig. 55) If you find that your grape has many wrinkles along the sides or bottom, it probably needs more stuffing. Use a toothpick or the point of a small pair of scissors to pack it full.

Draw the grape closed and sew around the gathered bottom again, picking up several of the outer pleats with a stitch, and pull to bring it into a smooth round shape. A few final stitches across the bottom will finish it.

Continue using the same thread to sew your grape into place. To be sure that the grape is securely fastened to the background, work from the top of the block, taking five or six stitches between the base of the grape and the background fabric to stitch it into place.

Small embellishments can change the look of this basic berry. Many berries will look more natural with a dimple in the top. Other variations may require even further detailing.

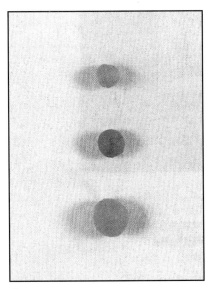

△ *Berry Sampler.*
Circle sizes for berries and flower buds:
small: dime; ¾" (19 mm)
medium: quarter; 1" (2.5 cm)
large: half dollar; 1¼" (3 cm)

▷ *Project #28: Grapes.*
Full size pattern on page 118.

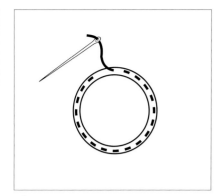

△ *Fig. 54. Circle of fabric. Turn a hem and stitch around edge.*

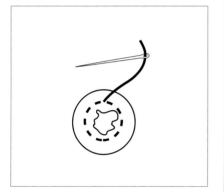

△ *Fig. 55. Pull to gather. Stuff and pull closed.*

PROJECT #29: BLUEBERRIES

Mark and cut medium and large fabric circles, referring to the samples for suggested sizes. These sizes will need no added seam allowance. Hem the circles and stuff as before. After the berry has been stuffed and sewn shut, take a stitch up through the top of the berry and back down again (Fig. 56), with the same thread, to form a dimple. Take the thread to the top again, and embroider a small circle around the dimple to make the perfect blueberry. (Fig. 57)

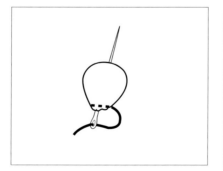

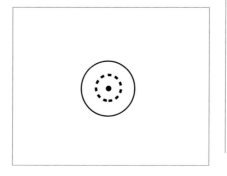

△ *Project #29: Blueberries. Full size pattern on page 119.*

◁ *Fig. 56. Stitch up through berry to make dimple on top.*

◁ *Fig. 57. Blueberry has circle embroidered around dimple.*

VARIATIONS ON BERRIES

PROJECT #30: LADYBUGS

With a little embellishment these free-form berries can become ladybugs. Make the basic stuffed berry from a bright red-orange fabric. Use a double ply of floss to add a stripe down the middle, a small triangular face, and dots on each side. (Fig. 58)

PROJECT #31: OPENING BUD

This gathered circle works equally well as a flower bud, either completely closed or just opening, with a bit of color showing. For the opening bud, turn the berry open end up and insert a small folded bud (Project #22) instead of the stuffing used to fill the grapes and berries. (Fig. 59)

To close this bud, stitch back and forth across the opening, hiding your thread in the gathers and catching the small folded bud as you stitch. Pull the thread down through the bud to the

△ *Project #30: Ladybugs.*
Full size pattern on page 120.

△ *Fig. 58. Ladybug embroidery.*

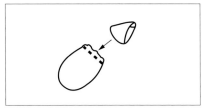

△ *Fig. 59. Turn berry open end up and insert a small folded bud.*

▷ *Project #31: Geranium.*
Full size pattern on page 121.

rounded end and then sew the bud in place, using the same thread.

BELLS
PROJECT #32: LILY-OF-THE-VALLEY

These little free-form flowers were inspired by bluebells discovered by Elly Sienkiewicz on a Baltimore Album quilt. I knew that, with a little adjustment, they were just what I needed to make my lily-of-the-valley blossoms.

Cut a rectangle 1" x 1¼" (2.5 cm x 3 cm) from white polished cotton. Fold in half crosswise, with right sides together. (Fig. 60) Sew a ⅛" (3 mm) seam up the side and take a back-stitch to end that seam. Continue sewing across the top, through both layers, with a ¼" (6 mm) seam and gather this line tightly, to create the cap of the flower. (Fig. 61) Tie off and cut the thread.

Turn the flower right side out, but do not push out corners on the cap. I have found that the easiest way to turn this little piece is to roll it over the point of a small pair of scissors or a white pencil. Fold up a generous hem to the inside, turning the raw edge up into the flower as far as it will go.

Leaving the knot at the seam on the outside of the flower, stitch a ³⁄₁₆" (5 mm) hem around the lower edge. I have found that slipping the flower over the end of a pencil will hold the hem in place and provide something to stitch against. When you have sewn completely around the hem, remove the flower from the pencil and pull the stitches to produce a little ruffle. (Fig. 62) If you find that your flower looks more like a berry, with very little ruffle at the bottom, take out the hem and sew it a little deeper.

Tie off your thread, but do not cut it. Use it to sew the flower into place, stitching back and forth between the seam of the flower and the back-ground block. Taking your last stitch directly into the top of the cap will make the flower bell out away from the stem.

A flower made in this style has many other possibilities. Think about other colors and other sizes for blue-bells, trumpet vine, etc.

See the photo of "Little Bit of Everything," page 47, for an example.

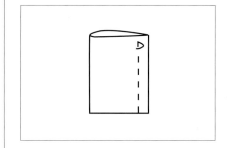

△ *Fig. 60. Stitch narrow ⅛" seam up side and backstitch at top.*

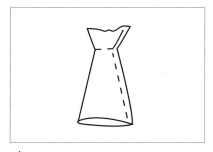

△ *Fig. 61. Gather across top, through both layers, making ¼" seam.*

△ *Fig. 62. Turn right side out. Fold hem to the inside and gather to make ruffled botttom.*

◁ *Project #32: Lily-of-the-valley. Full size pattern on page 122.*

RUCHING

Ruche (roosh) from the French: noun. a fluting or pleating of lace, ribbon, muslin, net, etc., for trimming dresses, especially at the wrist and neck.

Ruching was used as a trim on women's dresses through much of the nineteenth century. The Ohio Historical Society has in its collection a gray silk dress c. 1810 which has a ruched strip as an added embellishment around the collar. According to Ellice Ronsheim, curator of textiles, the ruching was done with an angled or "S" curved line of stitching along a folded strip of fabric.

Another type of ruched or wrinkled surface texture can be created by manipulating a single flat piece of fabric to fill an area of smaller dimensions.

In the mid-nineteenth century, when appliqué was at its high point, these same ruching techniques were adapted for use on quilts and evolved from a gathered strip or ruffle to flowers and other embellishments.

The following is a collection of ruched embellishments, some in the style of nineteenth century quilts and some that are completely new ideas.

BASIC STRIP RUCHING DIRECTIONS

Stitching which follows a zigzag line across a narrow strip produces the gathered, curved edges of this type of ruching. In the projects that fol-low, there are variations in the way that the strip is prepared, but the basic methods for marking and stitching are the same. All of the fabric strips that I use for ruching are cut on the bias. Bias gathers more easily, has more "give" for a softer look, and will not ravel.

Following are general directions for practice in making a ruched strip. Specific instructions will be given for each project.

Cut a 1½" (3.8 cm) wide bias strip, any length, and fold it lengthwise into thirds. Press to hold the folds in place, but do not baste. Place the strip wrong side up, along the edge of a ruler. Measure ½" (1 cm) in from the beginning of the strip and make a dot at the top edge. Continue to mark every 1" (2.5 cm) along the top edge. The last dot should be placed so that there is at least ½" (1 cm) left at the end of the strip. Along the bottom edge, measure 1" (2.5 cm) from the beginning and continue to mark every 1" (2.5 cm) to the end. The marks along the bottom should be offset from the marks at the top edge, as shown. (Fig. 63) The RucheMark™ ruching guide is a quick and accurate tool for marking ruching lines. See page 146.

It is important to use quilting thread for its strength when gathering this strip. Choose a matching color, as it will show a little. Begin by hiding your knot inside the fold, at the first dot along the top edge. Use a running stitch and sew through all of the layers to the next dot at the bottom edge. Continue to the next dot at the top edge and then pull on the thread to gather the fabric. You should see one "petal" formed by these two lines of stitching. At this point, hold the gathers firmly in place and take a back-stitch to secure this petal.

Throwing your thread over the

edge for this backstitch will create a sharp division between the petals. It will also make the thread more visible than a stitch taken behind the edge of the strip. I prefer the softer edge and hidden stitch, and so take my backstitch on top of the last gathering stitch instead of over the edge. Try it both ways on this sample piece to see the difference.

Stitch down to the next dot and up again to make another petal, pull tightly to gather, and backstitch again. Work your way along the strip to the last dot. (Fig. 64) Do not stitch completely to the end of the strip.

This ruched strip has possible uses as a textured vine or edging on flower petals. We will be looking at ways to create flowers and other embellishments by further manipulation of a ruched strip.

▽ *Fig. 63. Basic Strip Ruching.*
1½" bias strip, folded into thirds. Measure in ½" along top edge and mark. Mark every 1" along top. Measure in 1" along bottom edge and mark. Mark every 1" along bottom. To avoid having to measure, use the RucheMark™ ruching guide.

Metric.
3.8 cm wide bias strip, folded lengthwise into thirds. Measure in 1 cm along top edge and mark. Continue, marking every 2.5 cm along top edge. Measure in 2.5 cm along bottom edge. Continue to mark every 2.5 cm along bottom edge.

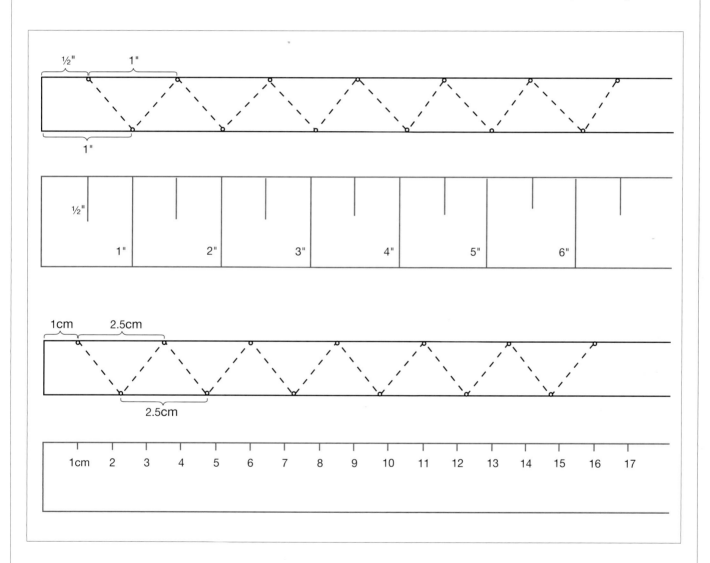

◁ *Project #38: Small Ruched Flower with Tufted Center. Full size pattern on page 126.*

▷ *Fig. 64. Gathering stitches sewn dot to dot and pulled tightly to form ruched strip.*

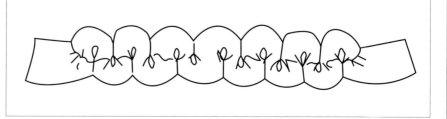

53

RUCHING FOR FREE-FORM EMBELLISHMENTS

PROJECT #33: SMALL RUCHED FLOWERS

Cut a bias strip 1¼" x 6" (3 cm x 15 cm) for each flower. Fold up ¼" (6 mm) at the bottom edge and press into place. Fold the top raw edge down, overlapping the bottom hem and press again.

Begin marking along the top, closed edge. Measure in ½" (13 mm) and make a dot. Continue to mark every 1" (2.5 cm) across the top edge five more times. You should have ½" (13 mm) of fabric left at the end of the strip.

Measure in 1" (2.5 cm) along the bottom edge and make a dot. Con-tinue to mark every 1" (2.5 cm) along the bottom edge four more times. (Fig. 65)

With quilting thread, gather from dot to dot, forming five petals along the top edge and four at the bottom. Working with this short strip, you may secure each petal with a backstitch as you work your way along the strip, or wait until the end to draw it up. Pull the gathers as tightly as you can. Tie off the thread, but do not cut it.

When the petals are made, lay the strip out flat and study it a moment. You will see that the edge with four petals has a half-petal at each end. (Fig. 66) These half petals are not needed in the flower and should be included in the seam allowance when the ends are joined.

Place the ends of the strip right sides together and, with the same thread, stitch across on the diagonal, as shown. (Fig. 67) Tie off and cut the thread. Open the flower out flat with the five petals to the outside. (See photo below.) Do not trim the seam allowances, but tuck them underneath the flower, to be hidden when it is sewn down.

These little flowers can be blind-stitched into place along the outside edge or just tacked into place through the gathers, leaving the edges free. Embroidered knots are a pretty way to tack down the center.

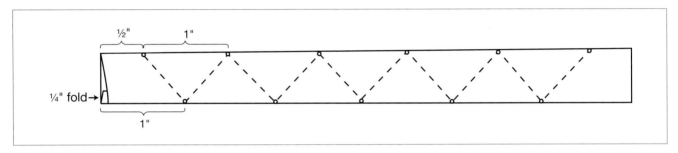

△ *Fig. 65. 1¼" x 6" bias strip marked for ruching.*

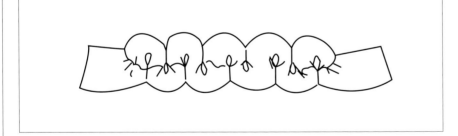

◁ *Fig. 66. Five petals on top, four petals on bottom, two half petals.*

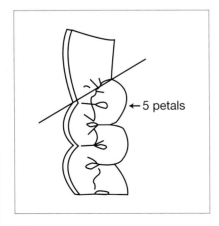

◁ 5 petals

◁ *Fig. 67. Join ends of strip. Right sides together. Sew on diagonal, with half petals in seam allowance.*

◁ *Project #33: Small Ruched Flowers. Full size pattern on page 98. Open with five petals to outside of flower. See photo on page 17 for entire block.*

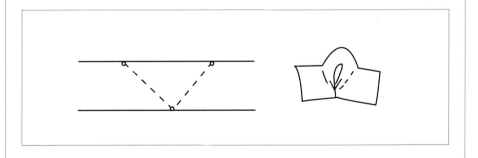

◁ *Project #34: Ruched Buds. Full size pattern on page 123.*

◁ *Fig. 68. 1¼" wide bias strip. Fold and mark for ruching; stitch one "v" for each petal.*

VARIATIONS

PROJECT #34: RUCHED BUDS

Flower buds can be made to accompany the small ruched flowers by making a similar ruched strip of only one, two, or three petals. (Fig. 68) Instead of bringing the ends together to form a full flower, simply turn the ends under and blindstitch all of the edges into place to form a bud.

COMPOSITE OR CLUSTER-TYPE FLOWERS

Some flowers, such as geraniums or hydrangea are really a grouping of smaller blossoms. This look can be created by using a dozen or so very small ruched flowers.

To eliminate the bulk of a folded strip, use a raw edge bias strip. Some fabrics will have a more stable raw edge than others; test the fabric that you plan to use. If you want a smooth edge, you can treat the fabric with Fray Check® or use ribbon instead. I have found silk ribbon especially beautiful to use.

PROJECT #35: GERANIUM

Cut a ½" x 4" (13 mm x 10 cm) bias strip. Mark the strip for ruching, as shown in the diagram. (Fig. 69) This will give you three petals across the top edge. Use quilting thread and stitch the strip for ruching without backstitching. Pull to gather. Join the ends, as you did with the other small ruched flowers. Look carefully to find and eliminate the small half petals. Trim away the excess seam allowance. If you have used ribbon, you may need to overcast the cut ends to prevent them from raveling.

Use three small embroidery knots in the center of each flower to hold it in place on the block. (Fig. 70) Use the geranium pattern as a guide for placement and assemble as many of these little blossoms as needed to fill in the flower.

STRIP VARIATIONS

With the proper manipulation, ruched strips can be used to create free-form embellishments other than flowers. The basic ruching pattern remains the same, but variations in the way that the strip is finished can produce different shapes.

PROJECT #36: RUCHED BUTTERFLY

This clever use for a ruched strip came from Lois K. Ide of Bucyrus, Ohio. I have made some minor changes in its construction. See the photo at left.

Cut a bias strip 1¼" x 4" (3 cm x 10 cm). Along the top edge, fold a ¼" (6 mm) hem to the wrong side and press into place. Fold the bottom raw edge up, overlapping the top hem and press again. Reversing the fold of this strip will make it easier to fold smooth points on the wing tips.

Mark the strip for ruching as shown. (Fig. 71) With quilting thread, gather from dot to dot. Do not back-stitch along this strip, so that you will have the freedom to adjust the gathers later. The strip should have three scallops on top and two on the bottom. (Fig. 72)

Lay the ruched strip down flat, right side up. You will see that this strip also has half-petals at each end. We will make good use of these partial petals in this little butterfly motif. Fold under the raw edge at one end of the strip. To make a pointed wing tip, fold the top corner in and down under the wing. (Fig. 73) Pull the wing tip up so that the wing curves gently from the last scallop out to the point. (Fig. 74) You may need to loosen the gathers slightly to make a smooth line across the top edge. Secure this wing into place on the block and repeat for the other side.

All three scallops across the top of the butterfly should come together to form the body and upper wings, and the two scallops at the bottom should be pulled apart to create the bottom wings. Appliqué around the entire butterfly with a blindstitch. Use embroidery stitches to add the body and antennae.

I put this little butterfly in the corner of my thistle block. You may want to make several and scatter them throughout your quilt.

◁ Project #35: Geranium.
Full size pattern on page 121.

◁ Project #36: Ruched Butterfly.
Full size pattern for Thistle on page 124.

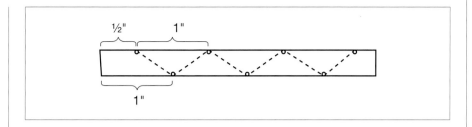

△ Fig. 69. ½" wide bias strip or ribbon. Ruche as shown.

◁ Fig. 70. Fasten in place with knots.

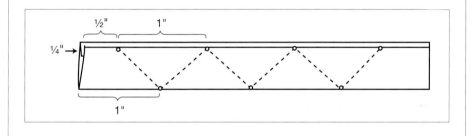

△ Fig. 71. 1¼" x 4" bias strip. Mark 7 dots for ruching.

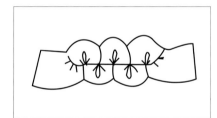

◁ Fig. 72. Three scallops on the top, two scallops on the bottom.

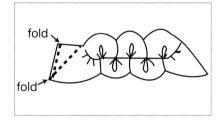

◁ Fig. 73. To shape wing tips: first, fold raw edge in. Second, fold top corner down.

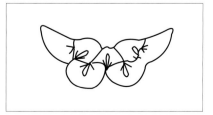

◁ Fig. 74. Pull corners up to form wings.

◁ *Project #37:* Ruched Pine Cones. *Full size pattern for Evergreen on page 125.*

▷ *Fig. 75.* Bias strip 1" x 9" folded in thirds. Mark for ruching as shown.

Project #37: Ruched Pine Cones

Cut a bias strip, 1" x 9" (2.5 cm x 23 cm) for a small cone. Fold the strip lengthwise into thirds, right side out, and press. Lay the strip wrong side up with the closed edge at the top and mark for ruching, as shown. The first five marks along the top of the strip will be placed on the top folded edge. At this point, the top fold of the strip is opened and the remaining marks are placed on the raw edge of the bottom hem. (Fig. 75) Mark every 1" (2.5 cm) along the bottom edge, as usual.

Begin sewing at the end of the strip with three layers of fabric. With quilting thread, gather from dot to dot, securing with a backstitch as you go. When you come to the point where the strip is opened up, continue to stitch, but only through the two-layer hem. Work to the end of the strip, but do not cut your thread. (Fig. 76)

Tucking the raw edge of the end of the strip inside, begin to roll and spiral the strip. Take tacking stitches through the entire body of the piece at each scallop, to hold it together. (Fig. 77) The scallops should spiral up the outside and the raw edges will fill the inside to give the pine cone dimension. As you work, take care to overlap the edges enough that the pine cone has a short and chubby shape, rather than long and spindly.

As you reach the top, you will find that the last four scallops also have finished edges on the top which will be used to cover any remaining raw edges and create a cap for the pine cone. A drawstring type of stitch works best here. Slide the needle through the fold along the top edge of each scallop and draw them tightly together. (Fig. 78) Use the remaining thread to stitch the pine cone into place on the evergreen block. A pattern and directions for working the evergreen branch are given in the embroidery section under Project #59 for straight stitch.

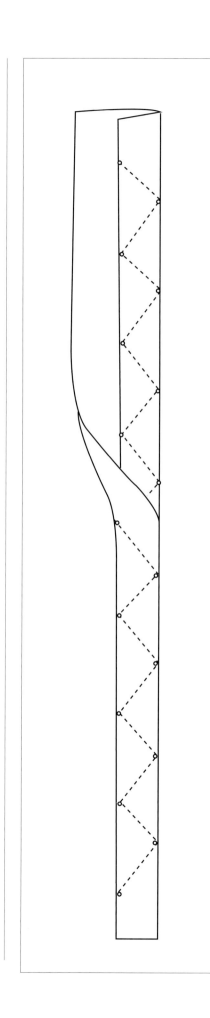

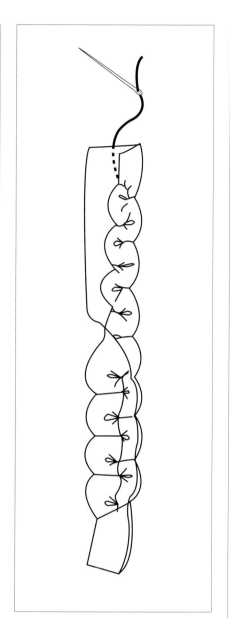

△ *Fig. 76. Ruched strip.*

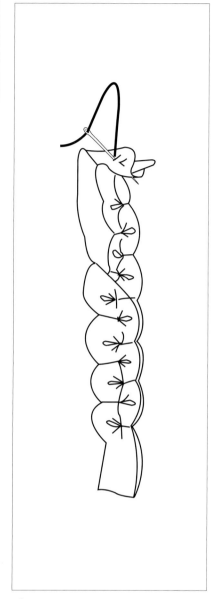

△ *Fig. 77. Begin to roll and spiral strip. Use same thread and tack through pine cone to hold all layers in place.*

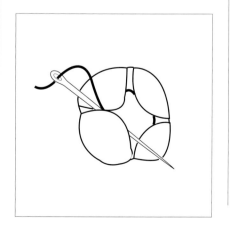

◁ *Fig. 78. Drawstring stitch to close top.*

EDGE RUCHING

There are perhaps unlimited variations in strip ruching. Changing the length or size of the strip will produce a different look. I have been able to create several different types of flowers by changing the size and fold of the strip and ruching only one edge.

PROJECT #38: SMALL RUCHED FLOWER WITH TUFTED CENTER

Cut a bias strip 1¼" x 6" (3 cm x 15 cm). Measure up ¼" (6 mm) from the bottom raw edge and mark a line along the length of the strip. With quilting thread, work a line of running stitches along this marked line. Begin and end the stitching ½" (13 mm) from each end. Leave both tails of thread on the right side of the fabric. This thread will be used later to draw up the center of the flower. (Fig. 79)

Press down a ½" (13 mm) hem along the top edge, toward the wrong side of the fabric. The raw edge should just meet the previously stitched line. Mark along this hem for ruching, in the basic strip ruching pattern. Stitch along the hem, gather, and then join the ends of the strip, as shown (Fig. 80), to form a five petaled flower. Turn the piece right-side out, so that the petals lie flat and the raw edges come up through the center of the flower. Find both ends of the gathering thread and pull to gather the center. (Fig. 81) Tie the threads securely and trim the ends.

Trim carefully around the raw edges of the flower center to create a slightly mounded shape and then rub the edges with your fingers to fray and soften the center. Trim away any stray threads.

PROJECT #39: LARGE FLOWER WITH RUCHED EDGE

Cut a bias strip 2¼" x 16" (5.7 cm x 41 cm). On the wrong side, measure ½" (13 mm) up from the bottom edge, and draw a line along the length of the strip. With quilting thread, sew a line of running stitches along this marked line. These stitches will be gathered later to form the center of the flower.

Press down a ½" (13 mm) hem along the top edge. Mark this hem for ruching along the top and bottom edges *of this hem only*. (Fig. 82)

Using quilting thread, gather from dot to dot, drawing up and securing each petal as you go. This will form the outside edge of the flower. When you reach the last dot, tie off your thread to secure the petals, but do not cut the thread. Bring both ends of

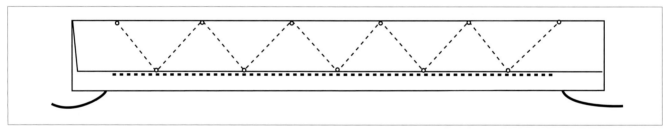

△ *Fig. 79. 1¼" x 6" bias strip. Thread tail left on right side of strip.*

△ *Project #38: Small Ruched Flower with Tufted Center. See photo page 52. Full size pattern on page 126.*

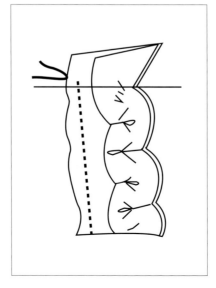

◁ *Fig. 80. Join ends, right sides together.*

△ *Fig. 81. Turn flower right side up, raw edges up through center. Pull threads to gather center and tie off. Trim center to shape.*

the strip right sides together and sew a seam across the ends to join them. (Fig. 83) Be careful not to catch the line of gathering stitches as you sew across it. When the ends are joined, tie and cut this thread.

Pull up both ends of the gathering thread to close the center of the flower. Raw edges should be to the wrong side. (Fig. 84) Pull tightly, but carefully, until the center closes, and tie the thread ends to hold the gathers in place. Depending on the weight of your fabric, the center may or may not close completely. If it does not close, wrap the ends of the gathering thread around the center in opposite directions to cinch it closed and tie again.

Spread out the center seam allowance so that it is evenly distributed and raises the center of the flower. Position the flower on the block and secure it in place with small tacking stitches within the gathers of each petal, allowing the edges to remain free.

The center must be secured with tacking stitches and may also be filled with an embellishment, such as embroidery or a "torn" center.

I have made this flower in two other sizes, beginning with strips cut 2" x 10" (5 cm x 25 cm) and 2" x 12" (5 cm x 30 cm). Feel free to experiment with others.

△ *Project #39: Large Flower with Ruched Edge. Full size pattern on page 127.*

▷ *Fig. 83. Join ends, right sides together.*

▷ *Fig. 84. Pull to gather center. Leave raw edges on wrong side.*

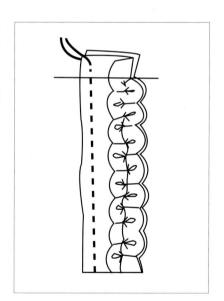

▽ *Fig. 82. Bias strip 2¼" x 16". Gather along line ½" from bottom edge; add ruching in ½" hem along top edge.*

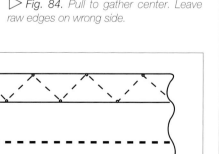
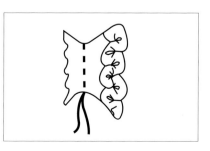

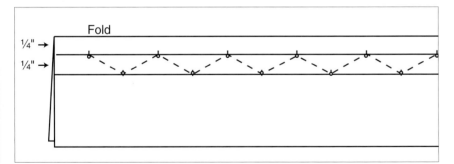

△ *Project #40: Daffodil.*
Full size pattern on page 128.

△ *Fig. 85. 3" x 8" bias strip. Fold in half lengthwise. Mark for ruching.*

PROJECT #40: DAFFODIL

The daffodil combines edge ruching with a unit appliqué technique similar to the daisy. The base petals are worked onto a layer of batting to help prevent shadow through. The trumpet is ruched and attached to create a complete flower that can be set into place as one piece.

Make a template for each base petal and cut the shapes from fabric with seam allowance all around each one. Allow an extra allowance at the center edge, so that the petals will come together beneath the free-form trumpet. Baste the seam allowances under and pin each petal into position on a thin layer of batting. Appliqué the

petals to each other where they overlap. Use a blindstitch and sew through the batting, just as if you were appliquéing the flower to the background block. Do not sew the outside edges to the batting.

DAFFODIL TRUMPET

This is somewhat like the lily-of-the-valley, but because of its size and open center it needs to be finished inside as well.

Cut a bias strip 3" x 8" (7.6 cm x 20 cm). Fold in half lengthwise, wrong sides together, and press. Measure down ¼" (6 mm) from the fold and draw a line along the length of the piece. Measure down ¼" (6 mm) from this first line and draw another line parallel to it. Mark for ruching between these lines, (Fig. 85) following the general ruching directions (page 52). Do not begin to sew yet.

Open the strip and place the ends right sides together, matching first and last dots. Sew a ½" (1 cm) seam to join the ends. (Fig. 86) Trim the seam to ¼" (6 mm) and finger press the seam open.

Fold the piece in half again along the pressed line, with the marks to the outside. Stitch ruching as marked around the whole trumpet. (Fig. 87) Use quilting thread, in a matching color, and leave the knot inside the fold. Do not backstitch on this piece. After the ruching is complete, adjust the fullness and tie off and cut the thread.

Use the same quilting thread to gather around the raw edge to form the base of the trumpet. (Fig. 88) This will not come completely closed, but will be hidden when the trumpet is sewn to the flower petals.

Blindstitch the trumpet onto the center of the base petals, stitching through the layer of batting. Trim away

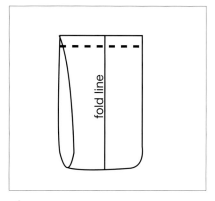

△ *Fig. 86. Open fold. Match first and last dots and stitch across ends, right sides together.*

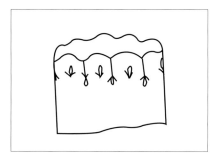

△ *Fig. 87. Re-fold on pressed line. Stitch through both layers for ruching.*

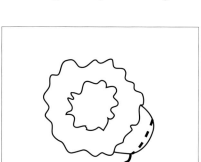

△ *Fig. 88. Gather base.*

▷ *Project #41: Iris.*
Full size pattern on page 129.

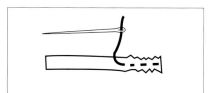

△ *Fig. 89. Stitch down center of ¼" or ⅜" wide bias strip.*

the excess batting around the outside edges of the flower.

Appliqué the finished flower into place on the prepared background. Sew around the outside edges and again at the base of the trumpet to hold it securely. Position the trumpet so it lies slightly to one side of the center and tack it into place, so that the joining seam is hidden.

STRAIGHT LINE RUCHING

For some embellishments, sewing a line of gathering stitches straight down the middle of the strip will produce the desired effect.

PROJECT #41: IRIS BEARD

This fuzzy little embellishment for an iris is made from a raw edge bias strip. Depending on the size of your flowers, cut a strip ¼" or ⅜" (1 cm) wide and about 3" (8 cm) long.

Using matching sewing weight thread, gather straight down the center of the strip and draw up tightly. (Fig. 89) Continue until the beard is as long as needed. Try to prevent the strip from twisting. Knot the thread to hold the gathers securely, but do not cut your thread. Use this same thread to stitch the beard into place on the flower petal, tacking through the gathered center line. Be sure to follow a slight curve in placement of the beard for a natural look. Use a small pair of scissors to trim the end of the beard to a point and soften the edges a little, by rubbing them between your fingers.

◁ *Project #42:* Caterpillar.
Full size pattern for Yarrow on page 136.

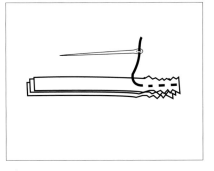

△ *Fig. 90. Three layers of ⅜" x 4" or ½" x 4" bias strips.*

PROJECT #42: CATERPILLAR

I have always enjoyed caterpillars and so they seemed a natural addition to my designs. To make this wooly worm, cut 3 bias strips ⅜" or ½" x 4" (1 cm x 10 cm). Layer the strips on top of each other and with quilting thread, gather them straight down the middle. (Fig. 90) Allow the strip to twist, as it will want to do. When you reach the end, pull to make sure that the gathers are tight, and then tie the thread and cut it off. Spread apart the layers of fabric and fray the edges with your fingers. This may be easier to do if the fabric is slightly damp. Twist the strip and rough up the edges as needed to make a nice fat caterpillar. (Fig. 91)

Some fabrics will fray out better than others. You may want to experiment with several. Solid color fabric or a print with color that carries through to the back seems to work best as both the right and wrong sides of the fabric will show. Layers of different colored fabrics will produce a striped caterpillar.

You will find my caterpillar on the embroidered yarrow block above.

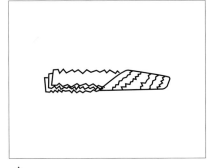

△ *Fig. 91. Twist strip, fray out edges.*

SURFACE TEXTURE

An entirely different type of ruching can be done by using a large flat piece of fabric instead of a strip. The texture is developed by wrinkling and tacking the fabric in order to make it fit into an area of smaller dimensions. This type of ruching has the potential for great variations in finished appearance, from a soft, loosely gathered surface to one that is very tight and textured. See photos on page 66.

Depending on the shape of the motif, cut a circle or rectangle with twice the dimensions as the space which you intend to fill. For example, a 1" circle would require a 2" circle of fabric, and a 2" x 3" flower would require a 4" x 6" piece of fabric.

The following are general directions for surface texture ruching and should be read through before starting the thistle project. If a practice piece is desired, cut a 3" (7.6 cm) circle of fabric and follow the directions to fit it onto a 1½" (3.8 cm) circle drawn onto a small piece of background fabric.

SAMPLE:

Baste a narrow hem around the edge of the appliqué fabric. Fold the piece to divide it into quarters and place a pin or mark in the hem at each fold. (Fig. 92) Since the appliqué piece has no real shape, you will need to have an accurately marked placement line on your background fabric. Put marks on this background placement line to divide it into quarter sections too. (Fig. 93) Pin the edges of the fabric piece onto the marked outline, matching the marks to distribute the fullness evenly. (Fig. 94) If the piece is very large, each quarter section should be divided into several smaller units and pinned into place.

With a blindstitch, sew the edges into place, taking a few gathering stitches in the edge of the hem as needed to ease in the fullness. (Fig. 95) As you work, be sure to follow the placement line marked on the background block. I usually make two appliqué stitches and then take one or two running stitches in the hem and pull to gather. Do not gather by sliding your needle through the fold of the hem, as there will be nothing to hold it in place after the basting is removed. Work only a small measured area at a time and keep an eye on the fabric remaining and the space left to cover, so that it comes out even. When you are finished appliquéing, remove the basting stitches from the hem.

There will be an excess of fabric standing up in the center of the motif, which now can be tacked into place to create beautiful texture.

Before starting to ruche the fabric, use a small pin or basting stitch in the center of the appliqué piece to secure it to the background and distribute the fullness evenly. Use a matching sewing weight thread to tack the fabric down, easing it into an evenly textured surface. Carry the thread along the back of the block and try to place the stitches down in the valleys that you are creating, not across any of the fabric that is raised from the surface. Take care not to pull the block out of shape with these longer stitches on the back. A larger piece may benefit from being placed in a hoop while this tacking is done.

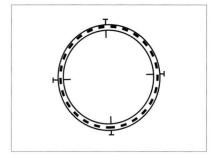

△ *Fig. 92. Divide circumference into quarters and mark with pins.*

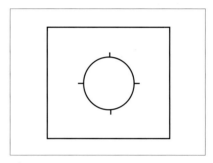

△ *Fig. 93. Divide background placement line into quarters.*

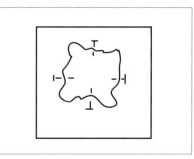

△ *Fig. 94. Pin fabric into place, distributing fullness evenly.*

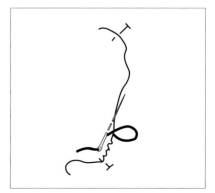

△ *Fig. 95. Alternate gathering and blindstitching to ease excess fabric into place.*

◁ *Suface texture examples:*
Lilacs and Carnations. Full quilt shown on page 93.

▷ *Evergreen and Chickadee* 1990, 14"
Made by Golda Lounsberry.
Designed by the author. Using as much embroidery as appliqué, this Christmas wreath was made by Golda Lounsberry of Harrow, Ontario. Techniques include corded and stuffed appliqué, unit appliqué chickadee and ribbon, free-form berries, and ruched pine cones.

PROJECT #43: THISTLE

Cut a 2" (5 cm) square of fabric for each thistle head. Trim to make the top edge a little narrower and to round off the lower corners. Baste the edges under. Use two or three pins to position the fabric so that the fullness will be evenly distributed.

Appliqué around the edge, alternating a blindstitch and a gathering stitch, as needed, to make the piece fit the marked placement line. Use a matching sewing weight thread.

Push the excess fabric down into soft folds and tack it into place to create the rough surface texture of the thistle head. Refer to the sections on fused leaves Project #21 and textured satin stitch Project #49 to finish this block.

▷ *Project #43: Thistle.*
Full size pattern on page 124.

EMBROIDERY EMBELLISHMENT

SUPPLIES & BASICS

Embroidery can be used to add rich embellishment and fine detail to appliqué work. If the stitches are well planned and delicately executed, the embroidery is not just surface decoration but becomes an integral part of the design.

The stitches that I use are few in number and simple to work. Much of the variety in the finished appearance comes from using different weights and types of thread, an assortment of fibers, and a good range of color. I may work with a single thread for fine detail, a double ply or textured thread for a heavier line, or two colors worked together for a special effect.

It is important to know which type of thread and which stitch will create the desired look. Sewing threads will produce a clean hard line, while floss is softer, sometimes fuzzy. Pearl cotton, silk twist, and crewel or needle-point wool add texture. Silk and rayon sewing threads have beautiful sheen and metallics can be used for sparkle.

Threads worked on top of an appliqué motif can be lighter or darker than the fabric to add visual interest to the piece, or they can be of a matching color and value for adding texture only. Two colors can also be worked together to add depth and shading or to create another color.

THREADS

EXTRA FINE

A very fine thread, such as a machine embroidery thread, can be used to work the most delicate of details. Try using it in a matching color for fine veins in petals or leaves, where it will add texture without calling attention to itself. Outlining a motif with a thread just slightly darker than the appliqué fabric will create a shadow line, setting it off from the background. This very fine weight also works beautifully in a blanket stitch around the edges of chintz appliqué.

SEWING THREAD

A standard sewing weight thread can also be used to produce a fine hard line for leaf or petal veins. It is slightly heavier, but is available in a full color range and is more likely to match the fabric. Often it can be the same thread that was used for the appliqué. Using a matching thread creates texture, without color or value contrast. A thread that is lighter or darker than the fabric will add more visual interest. Study the leaf or flower that you are trying to create to discover what kind of detail is needed.

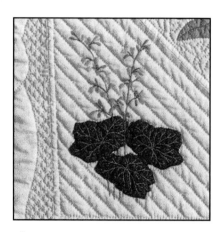

◁ *Extra Fine Thread Example.*
Dogwood Blossoms. Full quilt shown on page 92.

△ *Sewing Thread Example.*
Coral Bells, leaf veins. Full quilt shown page 93.

△ *Cotton Embroidery Floss Example.*
Flowers in vase. Full quilt shown page 93.

COTTON EMBROIDERY FLOSS

Embroidery floss has many applications. When used in line stitches, such as stems or tendrils, it produces a slightly heavier line, with a softer, somewhat fuzzy appearance. Floss will also give more body to single stitches, such as knots or daisy stitches. Because of its weight and smooth texture, it is a good choice for filling an area with satin stitch. Cotton floss comes in a six-ply strand. These plies should be separated and used one or two at a time.

PEARL COTTON #3, #5, #8, #12

Pearl cotton is a very textured thread with a marked twist and a soft sheen. It comes in several sizes with the larger number being the finer weight. Pearl cotton can be couched into place or it can be worked through the fabric.

Because of the heavy twist of the thread, pulling it through a tightly woven fabric may cause it to twist and knot. However, the beautiful texture of pearl cotton worked in a stem stitch is worth the effort involved.

WOOL

I found wool embroidery thread used throughout the Follett House album quilt and have seen it on other quilts made in the mid-nineteenth century. It was used in the Follett House quilt as an appliqué thread which matched in color but added texture to the edges of many leaves and flowers. Wool in a contrasting color was used for outlines and details in flower petals and centers. Crewel wool has a rough, slightly ragged texture, while needle-point wool has a smoother finish.

△ *Pearl Cotton Thread Example.*
Name plate. Full quilt shown page 92.

▷ *Wool Thread Example.*
Follett House Style Block. Made by the author.

SILK EMBROIDERY THREAD

Silk floss has a soft texture and a smooth luster. It is easy to work and produces a beautiful finish in line or filling stitches. Be aware as you make your choices that some silk threads are labeled "dry clean only." Silk itself is very washable, but can shrink and may or may not be colorfast.

SILK TWIST

Silk twist is softer and somewhat finer than pearl cotton. It has a visible texture and a beautiful sheen. Silk twist is used most often in crazy quilt work, but can add beautiful detail when used for lines, knots, and filling stitches in traditional appliqué.

SILK AND RAYON THREAD

Silk and rayon sewing weight threads are fine and soft. Both will work into a very fine line with a soft sheen. They are also beautiful when worked as a solid buttonhole edging for chintz appliqué.

METALLIC

To add a bit of sparkle, metallic thread may be used alone or as a blending filament worked in combination with other threads. Some metallic threads have a rough surface and may drag a little when worked through the fabric. Working with a shorter length of these threads will reduce the problem of fraying. Metallics are available in gold, silver, and a small range of colors.

TOOLS

Working with a variety of threads will require the use of different types of needles, such as sharps, crewels, and embroidery needles. I prefer to embroider with a fine needle and whenever possible, I use the same #12 sharp that I use for appliqué. This fine needle allows me to make very small stitches. The eye is small and for the most part will take only a single thread or floss. A double ply of floss can be worked with this fine needle by threading a single ply and pulling it through to double it. Working with two colors of floss, or a heavier thread will require the use of a needle with a larger eye, such as a #8 or #9 sharp or an embroidery needle which has a longer eye. A crewel needle is a larger embroidery needle used for heavier threads. Keep in mind that the size of the needle must be as large as the thread in order to make a hole in the fabric through which the thread can easily be pulled.

A needle which is the same diameter from eye to point area is a good choice for making knots.

Scissors for embroidery work should be small and very sharp. It is important to cut the ends of the threads cleanly for ease in threading. Small scissors are also easier to control when trimming thread ends close to the fabric.

Embroidery may be done with or without a hoop. I am able to maintain an even tension for most line stitches without a hoop. Quite often I am working through more than one layer of fabric, embroidering through an appliqué motif, and this adds stability to the piece. Some stitches such as a chain stitch which is pulled tightly, need the tension of a hoop to keep the fabric from being distorted. Stab stitches such as straight stitch, seed stitch, and knots are more easily worked if the fabric is supported in a hoop. I have also found that my satin stitch is more even if I work it as a stab stitch with the fabric stretched in a hoop.

◁ *Silk Embroidery Thread Example.*
Candle flames.

◁ *Silk, Rayon Thread Example.*
Chintz Appliqué. Full block photo shown page 84. Pattern not included.

△ *Metallic Thread Example.*
Pansy Block. Made by Janet Hamilton.
No pattern given.

BEGINNING AND ENDING A LINE

Begin the line of embroidery with a knot left on the back of the work. Often this knot can be hidden behind an appliqué piece. If the line also ends within the appliqué, it is a simple matter to take the thread to the back and tie it off in the same manner as an appliqué thread. If the embroidery line ends away from the appliqué as a vine or tendril might do, it will require more care in finishing. Take the thread to the back of the fabric and take a stitch or two under the last embroidery stitches and tie it off as usual.

Take care not to carry threads for any distance across the back of the block. Most often the embroidery threads will be of a darker value than the fabric and may shadow through.

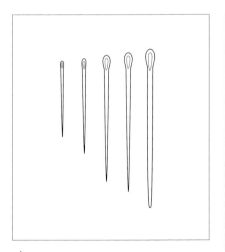

△ *Needle types.*
1. *Between – for quilting*
2. *Sharp – for appliqué*
3. *Embroidery (long eye)*
4. *Crewel (larger eye for wool)*
5. *Tapestry (blunt)*

◁ *Project #44: Snowflake. Full size pattern on page 130.*

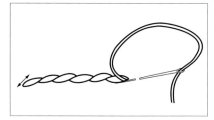

△ *Fig. 96. Outline stitch, a smooth line stitch. Needle faces in opposite direction, if you are right-handed, the thread will be above the line and stitches will lie SW to NE*

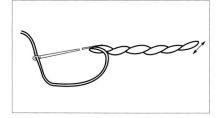

△ *Fig. 97. Outline stitch. If you are left-handed, the thread will be below the line.*

LINE STITCHES

OUTLINE STITCH

The outline stitch is a smooth line stitch that is worked through the fabric. The needle points in the opposite direction from the way that the line is actually being worked, so that it seems as if the needle is backing up with each stitch.

Begin at the left end of the line, if you are right-handed. Bring the needle up through the fabric, leaving a knot on the back. Take it down approximately ⅛" (3 mm) to the right, and come up halfway between these two places. The size of the stitch will vary with the weight of the thread. The next stitch again moves to the right and the needle, pointing left, comes up in exactly the same hole made by the previous stitch. Working the stitch into the same hole as the stitch before will help to produce a straight line. As you work, hold your loop of thread above the needle. (Fig. 96) This will give you a very smooth line.

If you are left-handed you will want to start at the right end of the line. The steps are the same, but hold the loop of thread below the needle as you work. (Fig. 97) The slant of the stitches should be SW to NE for both right- and left-handed work.

Use this stitch to outline shapes. It will create a shadow outline to set off pieces with little value contrast from the background or from other matching pieces, such as flower petals.

PROJECT #44: SNOWFLAKES

Appliqué these snowflakes into place. Use a fine thread of a slightly darker value to outline all of the edges and to set them off from the background. Work in a direction that will produce a smooth stitch, and will also throw the loop of thread against the edge of the appliqué. For right- or left-handers, this would be counterclockwise. Working with the loop of thread toward the appliqué will push the stitch more tightly against the edge.

STEM STITCH

The stem stitch is another line stitch, but worked in a slightly different way to give it more texture. As with the outline stitch, the needle faces in the opposite direction. The stitch is made in the same way, but the thread is held below the needle for right-handers (Fig. 98) and above for left-handers (Fig. 99) so that the slant of the stitches is NW to SE.

PROJECT #45: SPIDER WEB

Practice the stem stitch on the spider web. My own web was worked with extra-fine thread combined with a pearlized blending filament for glisten. I wanted very little value contrast between the web and the background, so that it would catch the viewer's eye only when positioned just right. Quilting will add a little more texture to this area.

Almost all types of thread have twist. Working a stitch which falls in line *with* the twist will produce a smooth line while a stitch which is worked *against* the twist creates texture. To see the difference, try working a sample of the outline and stem stitches with pearl cotton. You will see the effect more clearly with a highly textured thread. Be aware that some threads, such as pearl rayon, have an opposite twist and must be handled in the opposite way. This sounds confusing, but once you have worked a sample you will recognize the difference immediately. I like the texture produced by the stem stitch and use it most often for stems, leaf veins, and other lines.

Sewing around a circle or tight curve can pose a problem, since a straight line will touch a circle at only one point. Because these line stitches overlap each other, one stitch will help to hold the next one in place. When stitching around a tight curve, work in a manner that will give you a smooth or a textured line, as preferred, and at the same time, throw the thread toward the *outside* of the circle. If you are working with a textured line, you will need to work a circle in a counter-clockwise direction. Taking smaller stitches will also help create a smooth curve. If you find that you still have some straight looking stitches around a tight curve, go back and couch them into place. This is not cheating; it is simply tidying up.

△ *Fig. 98. Stem stitch, right-handed. A textured line stitch. Needle faces in opposite direction, thread is below line, stitches lie NW to SE.*

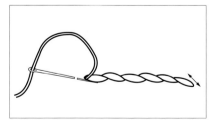

△ *Fig. 99. Stem stitch, left-handed. Thread is above line.*

▷ *Project #45: Spider Web. Full size pattern on page 131.*

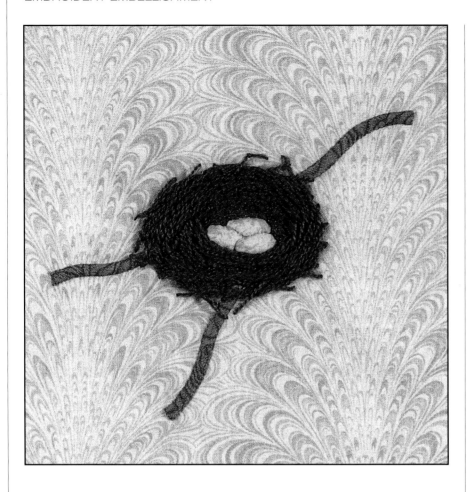

◁ *Project #46:* Bird's Nest.
Full size pattern on page 132.

CHAIN STITCH

Another line stitch I use quite often is the chain stitch. For this stitch the needle faces in the direction of the work. It will work the same right- or left- handed. Turn the work to whatever position is comfortable. I find that I get the best line if I work the stitches up and away at a slight angle.

The first stitch comes up and goes back into the same hole, and the needle advances slightly beneath the fabric. Catch the loop of thread under the point of the needle as it comes up, to prevent the stitch from falling through. (Fig. 101) This will give you a small tear-drop shaped loop of thread on the surface. For the next stitch, insert the needle into the fabric inside the previous loop stitch, as close as possible to the same hole. Catch the loop of thread under the needle and repeat the process until you have worked the entire line. Use a single stitch to couch over the last loop.

A chain stitch will give you a more textured line than an outline or stem stitch. It can be worked with multiple plies of floss to produce a line which is wider but not bulky. I prefer to work my chain stitch with small stitches and to pull them fairly tight so that they are textured but not open and lacy. (Fig. 102)

The chain stitch works especially well for lines with tight loops or turns such as tiny vines and tendrils. Because one stitch controls the placement of the next, it does not cause the jagged curve that a stem stitch sometimes does. The chain stitch is also a good choice for stems on leaves, fruits, and some delicate flowers.

COUCHING

Couching is the technique of laying one thread on the surface of the fabric and holding it in place by stitching over it with another. (Fig. 100) It can be used to create a straight line, without the texture of a stem or outline stitch. Couching is also a good choice for a thread that is too heavy to be worked through the fabric. The surface thread may be of any weight. The couching thread which holds it in place should be fine and of a matching color, unless contrast is desired.

PROJECT #46: BIRD'S NEST.

I couched down the lines of crewel wool which form the interior of this bird's nest in order to make it more recessed and to create a smoother surface on which to appliqué the eggs. The rim of the nest was worked with long straight stitches for more texture and dimension. Work these raised lines around the center first and then build toward the outside, overlapping the end of each one with the next.

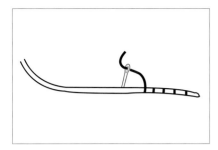

△ *Fig. 100. Couching. One thread is laid on surface and another thread is used to hold it in place.*

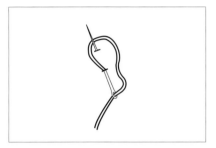

△ *Fig. 101. Chain Stitch. Needle faces direction of work. Needle goes down through same hole thread came up, and then comes up again, catching a loop of thread under its tip.*

△ *Fig. 102a. Chain Stitch. Left open, this stitch is lacey.*

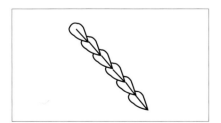

△ *Fig. 102b. Chain Stitch. Pulled closed, this stitch makes a textured solid line.*

PROJECT #47: HIBISCUS

Both the stem and the pistil of this flower are worked with a chain stitch, using two plies of floss. Match the color of the pistil to the color of the flower. For a more interesting texture and color, combine a single ply of green floss with a single ply of the flower color to work the stem.

▽ *Trendril Example. Grape Vine. Full quilt shown on page 93.*

▽ *Project #47: Hibiscus. Full size pattern on page 133.*

75

◁ *Project #48: Butterfly.*
Full size pattern page 134.

△ *Fig. 103. Satin Stitch.*
Long stitches laid side by side, and worked in same direction.

FILLING STITCHES

SATIN STITCH

The satin stitch uses long stitches laid side by side to fill an area. (Fig. 103) Each stitch should be worked in the same direction, for example, from the inside of a motif to the outside, to insure a smooth finish. To see if you are doing this correctly, turn the piece over. The stitches on the back should look almost the same as the front.

To produce the smoothest surface, there should be no twist or overlap in the threads. They should lie perfectly flat.

For best effect, these long stitches should follow the contours of the motif. You will occasionally need to add short fill-in stitches to change

the angle of the work. (Fig. 104)

PROJECT #48: BUTTERFLY

Butterfly wings are beautiful when done in satin stitch. Working an area like this with a fine silk or cotton floss, creates a smooth and lustrous appearance.

Begin by transferring the outline and all of the wing markings onto a piece of solid color fabric. Remember that this fabric will be what shows through as the larger wing spots and should be a bright accent color.

When the marking is complete, appliqué the butterfly into place, turning the seam allowances under all around. Do not worry about the body,

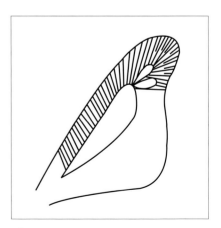

△ *Fig. 104. Shorter Satin Stitch.*
Short fill-in stitches help change the angle to follow contours.

as it will be added later with embroidery. The appliqué stitching does not have to be fine, as the entire edge will be covered by embroidery, but do turn the edge. Working the satin stitch over this raised edge instead of a flat edge adds a great deal of dimension to the finished piece.

Use an outline or stem stitch (your choice) and a single ply of floss to work all of the veins of the wings. These stitches should be in place before the edges are worked.

The satin stitch in the shaded areas of the wings is worked with a double ply of floss. Begin your stitch by bringing the needle up as close as possible to the vein lines that you have just stitched. Carry the thread over the outer edge of the wing, and take the needle down through the background fabric. Be sure to change the angle of your stitches as you fill

each area. I have found that placing the fabric in a hoop and working the satin stitch with an up and down stab stitch eliminates the distortion that can be caused by carrying the stitch across the underside in one motion.

TEXTURED SATIN STITCH

Another filling stitch which I have been using in my work for a while is one I call textured satin. It is similar to several other filling stitches. The stitches lie on the surface and have the sheen of a satin stitch. The long, but broken line of stitches looks something like long and short, but is worked in a different way.

A side view of the work will show that this is a line stitch, much like outline or stem. However, the top stitches are long and the catch stitch into the fabric is very short. (Fig. 105)

To begin, work a line of these

stitches along one edge of the area to be filled, turn the work around and stitch another line as close as possible to the first. Holding the loop of thread toward the area already worked will help it to fill completely. Continue to work lines back and forth, always holding the thread toward the area that is finished. The short catch stitches should be randomly placed to avoid developing a regular pattern. (Fig. 106)

This stitch is more economical than a traditional satin stitch because almost all of the thread used shows on the surface. Because it is worked completely from the top it can be worked over padded appliqué without flattening the piece. This stitch has wonderful texture and can look feathery or furry. Because it is an interrupted line, it is directional and can be used for contouring.

▽ *Textured Satin Stitch Example.*
Squirrel. Full quilt shown on page 93.

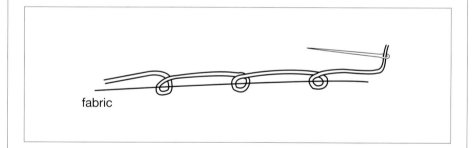

fabric

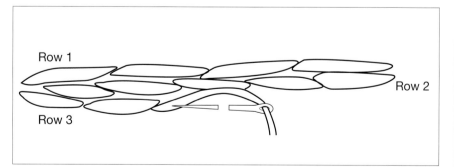

Row 1

Row 2

Row 3

△ *Fig. 105. (Top) Side view of Textured Satin Stitch. Long stitch on surface (¼" to ½"), short back stitch to hold it in place. Worked like rows of stem stitch; needle faces opposite.*

△ *Fig. 106. Close-up of Textured Satin Stitch. Stitches should be taken randomly to avoid a regular pattern. Hold loop of thread toward area already worked.*

PROJECT #49: THISTLE BLOSSOM

Use a single ply of floss and work lines as marked to fill in the thistle blossom. Be sure to add some short stitches to change angle as you work across to the other side. When the blossom has been filled, add a few separate stitches along the top edge for a soft, delicate finish.

TEXTURED SATIN STITCH ON PADDED APPLIQUÉ
PROJECT #50: HUMMINGBIRD

Use this hummingbird to see how embroidery detail can be added to the surface of a padded appliqué without stitching through to the background block. Appliqué the bird as one piece over a layer of batting. Work the colorful areas with a single ply of cotton floss and the textured satin stitch. Work only in the surface layer of the appliqué, so that the stitches do not flatten the piece.

◁ *Project #49: Thistle Blossom.*
Full size pattern on page 124.

◁ *Project #50: Hummingbird.*
Full size pattern on page 135.

◁ *Project #51:* Colonial Knot Daisy.
Full size pattern page 113.

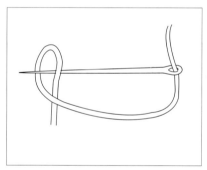

△ *Fig. 107.* French Knot.
Hold needle horizontally; wrap loop of thread over end of needle.

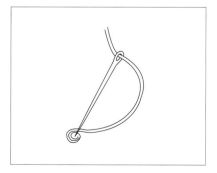

△ *Fig. 108.* French Knot.
Insert needle back into fabric, close to where thread came up but not in same hole.

KNOTS

Knots can be used as a filling stitch to add surface texture to an area or can be worked as individual stitches to add detail. I use them most often as flower centers. Use a hoop to support the fabric, so that both hands will be free to work above and below the block.

FRENCH KNOT

A French knot with a single wrap is a quick stitch to make and a good choice if you need a large number of knots. Simply take hold of the thread as it comes up from the fabric and wrap it around the point of the needle. (Fig. 107) Pull on the thread to tighten the knot and take the point of the needle back into the fabric, close to where the thread came up. (Fig. 108)

Extra wraps may be added, but the knots tend to become unruly with two or three wraps. The size of the knot may also be changed by changing the weight or number of plies of thread.

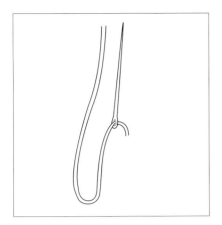

△ *Fig. 109a. Colonial Knot, right-handed. Hold the needle and thread parallel with the tip of the needle pointing toward the material.*

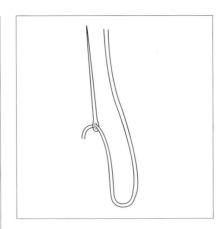

△ *Fig. 109b. Colonial Knot, left-handed.*

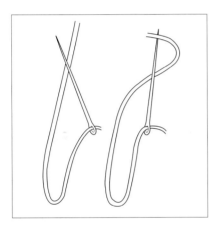

△ *Fig. 110a. Colonial Knot, right-handed. Cross the needle over the thread and continue in a counter clockwise motion taking the point of the needle underneath the thread, making the first wrap.*

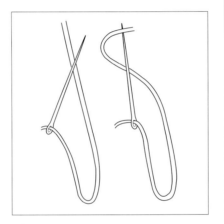

△ *Fig. 110b. Colonial Knot, left-handed. Cross the needle over the thread and continue in a clockwise motion taking the point of the needle underneath the thread, making the first wrap.*

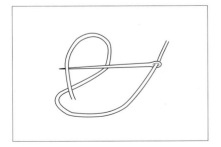

△ *Fig. 111a. Colonial Knot, right-handed. Hold the needle out parallel to the fabric.*

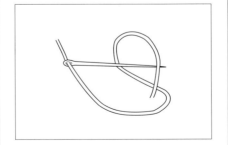

△ *Fig. 111b. Colonial Knot, left-handed.*

COLONIAL KNOT

I prefer to use this figure eight knot instead of a French knot because it seems to behave better, giving me a smoothly tied knot that lies close to the surface almost every time. It may take a little practice to memorize the necessary steps, but the results will be well worth the effort.

Take the thread in one hand and needle in the other. Hold them parallel to each other with the tip of the needle pointing toward the material. (Fig. 109a or b) Cross the needle over the thread and continue the circular motion taking the point of the needle underneath the thread, making the first wrap. (Fig. 110a or b) Turn the needle to a horizontal position. (Fig. 111a or b) Wrap the thread over and around the point of the needle to create a figure eight wrap. (Fig. 112a or b) Place the point of the needle into the fabric, close to, but not in the hole where the thread comes out. With the needle halfway through the fabric, pull on the thread to tighten the knot. (Fig. 113a or b) This figure eight wrap will hold itself in place if you let go of the thread to reposition your hands. Draw the needle through the knot and to the back of the fabric. An extra wrap may be added to the second half of this stitch to produce a slightly larger knot. Variations in size can also be obtained by changing the weight or ply of thread.

PROJECT #51: DAISY CENTER

Use a single ply of floss and either French or Colonial knots to create the fine texture of this daisy center. (Photo shown on pages 38 and 79.)

PROJECT #52: YARROW

Use a double ply of floss and the Colonial knot to work the large texture blossoms of the yarrow.

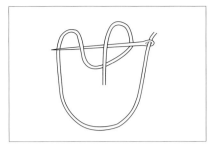

△ *Fig. 112a. Colonial Knot, right-handed. Wrap the thread over and around the point of the needle to create a figure eight wrap.*

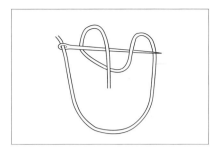

△ *Fig. 112b. Colonial Knot, left-handed.*

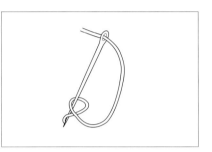

△ *Fig. 113a. Colonial Knot, right-handed. Place the point of the needle into the fabric, close to but not in the same hole the thread comes out. With the needle halfway through the fabric, pull on the thread to tighten the knot. Then draw the needle through the knot and to the back of the fabric.*

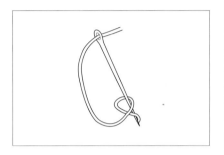

△ *Fig. 113b. Colonial Knot, left-handed.*

▷ *Project # 52: Yarrow.*
Full size pattern on page 136.

◁ *Project #53: Daylily.*
Full size pattern on page 137.

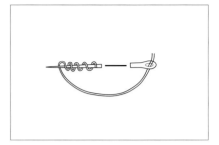

△ *Fig. 114. Bullion Knot. Stop halfway through; wrap thread around point of needle.*

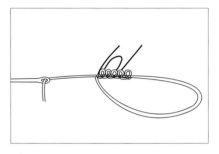

△ *Fig. 115. Bullion Knot. Hold wraps with finger and pull needle through.*

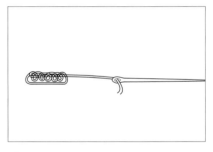

△ *Fig. 116. Bullion Knot. Reverse direction of pull to lay stitch in place.*

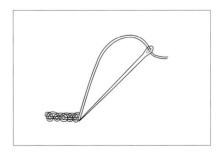

△ *Fig. 117. Bullion Knot. Take needle down through hole made by first stitch.*

BULLION KNOT

Another knot I especially like is the Bullion knot. It is long rather than round and can be made in a variety of sizes.

It is helpful to begin with a marked line to show the length and placement of the knot. With a little experience these can be done by eye. Bring the needle up at one end of the marked stitch and pull the thread through. Insert the needle at the other end of the marked line and bring it out at the first end again, stopping with the needle halfway through the fabric. Take hold of the thread near the point of the needle and wrap the thread around the point a number of times, until the length of the wraps looks equal to the length of the stitch line. (Fig. 114)

Hold these wraps of thread firmly in place with your finger or thumb and pull the needle through. (Fig. 115) The knot will be made, but will be lying in the wrong direction. When the knot feels firmly tied, reverse the direction of your pull to lay the knot into place. (Fig. 116) Finish the knot by taking your needle down through the hole made by the stitch already in place. (Fig. 117)

PROJECT #53: DAYLILY

For a practice piece, appliqué this daylily or another open flower. Use a double ply of floss and a chain stitch to embroider the heavy pistil in the center of the flower. Work the stamens with a single ply of floss and a stem stitch. Add the fuzzy anthers at the ends of the stamens with Bullion knots in a darker color, using a double ply of floss to make stitches ⅛" (3 mm) long and wrapped six times.

◁ *Uncle Sam, 1992, 20"x 27"*
Made by Jo Ann Lischynski.
This folk art Uncle Sam was designed and made by Jo Ann Lischynski, using the blanket stitch over a raw edge.

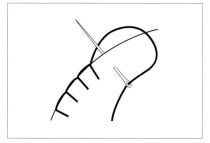

△ *Fig. 118. blanket stitch. With needle perpendicular to edge of appliqué, stitch goes down through appliqué and background fabric. Needle comes up through background at edge of appliqué and loop of thread is caught under needle.*

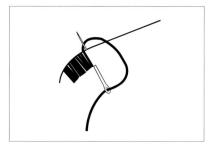

△ *Fig. 119. Buttonhole for chintz appliqué. Worked same as blanket stitches; stitches lie next to each other for solid edging.*

▽ *Project #54: Folk Art Bird. Full size pattern on page 138.*

EDGE STITCHES

BUTTONHOLE

The blanket stitch is an edge stitch which has great variety in application and finished appearance. It can be worked over a raw edge or a turned edge.

Begin this stitch by coming up from behind the block, just at the edge of the appliqué. Take the needle down through the appliqué, and with the needle perpendicular to the edge, come up through the background fabric, just at the edge of the appliqué. Catch the loop of thread under the needle, so that it will run from stitch to stitch along the outside edge. (Fig. 118) The stitches may be placed very close together for a satin type edge, or spaced further apart. The width of the stitches should remain even, as should the spacing between them.

For a folk art look, try using a single or double ply of floss worked in an open blanket stitch over a raw edge. A more sophisticated look can be achieved by using silk or rayon thread worked in a close stitch for chintz appliqué. (Fig. 119)

PROJECT #54: FOLK ART BIRD

Use a double ply of cotton floss to work an open blanket stitch over the raw edge of this bird wing.

◁ *Project #55: Chintz Appliqué.*
Pattern not included; use shapes in the print fabric..

PROJECT #55: CHINTZ APPLIQUÉ

Cut a printed motif from fabric. If desired, set the motif into place with a fusible bonding material. Use a single ply of silk or rayon thread to work a fine close blanket stitch around the edge.

REVERSE BUTTONHOLE

A different look is produced when the blanket stitch is reversed, with the closed edge against the appliqué and the open edge worked out into the background fabric. (Fig. 120) You might think about using this for the edges of leaves or ferns.

PROJECT #56: LEAVES OF FOLLETT HOUSE FLOWER

Use a single ply of floss to work the reverse blanket stitch against the turned edge of this leaf. I found it easier to maintain the slant of the stitches if I worked both sides of the leaf from the tip to the base.

◁ *Project #56: Leaves of Follett House Flower. Full size pattern on page 102.*

▷ *Project #57: Forget-Me-Nots. Full size pattern on page 139.*

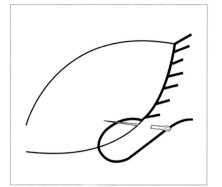

△ *Fig. 120. Reverse blanket stitch. Work against finished edge of appliqué needle perpendicular or slightly slanted. Stitch goes into background short distance from appliqué and comes up at edge of appliqué. Catch loop of thread under needle.*

△ *Fig. 121. Daisy Stitch. Left open. Single chain stitch; couch over loop to hold in place.*

△ *Fig. 122. Daisy Stitch. Pulled closed.*

△ *Fig. 123. Daisy Stitch. Filled with straight stitch for a wider solid stitch (fruit seeds).*

SINGLE STITCHES

DAISY STITCH

The daisy stitch is a single chain stitch held in place by a couching stitch over the end of the loop. Be sure to begin and end in the same hole so that the pointed end of the stitch will be closed. As with the chain stitch, this single loop may be left open (Fig. 121) or pulled closed (Fig. 122). It may also be filled with another stitch for a wider, solid look. (Fig. 123)

Use an open stitch for small flower petals and the closed or filled stitch for fruit seeds.

PROJECT #57: FORGET-ME-NOTS

These little blossoms are made with a grouping of four or five daisy stitches worked from a common center point. Use a double ply of floss to give some body to the petals. Finish each flower with a knot in the center.

SEED STITCH

A seed stitch can be a single short stitch (Fig. 124) or two stitches which begin in the same hole and end beside each other. (Fig. 125) The finished look is that of a short broad stitch which can be used for flower centers or fruit seeds.

PROJECT #58: STRAWBERRIES

Work a series of seed stitches into the surface of padded strawberries to create natural looking texture. Use one ply of floss and short single stitches.

STRAIGHT STITCH

As its name implies, this is a straight line produced by a single stitch. A straight stitch will produce a very fine line, without the texture of a stem or outline stitch. The thread simply comes up at one end of the stitch and is carried across the fabric to the other end. (Fig. 126a and b) Because the thread lies loosely on the surface, there is a practical limit to the length of these stitches.

PROJECT #59: EVERGREEN NEEDLES

Choose floss in closely related greens in light, medium, and dark values, plus a rusty brown, to work the evergreen branch.

Use one ply each of rusty brown and dark green floss, in the same needle, to work a chain stitch along the main branches of the evergreen. Use a single ply of a medium green and a stem stitch to work all of the side stems drawn on the pattern.

The evergreen needles have not been drawn on the pattern, and are added by eye after the main branches and side stems have been worked. Use one ply each of light green and dark green floss in the same needle to add straight stitches as shown. (Fig. 127) Notice that the needles grow in a "v" shape toward the tip of the stem. Because most quilters have an obsession with tiny stitches, there is always a tendency to make these stitches too short. Be generous here, making stitches that are about ¼" (6 mm) long, for lush branches. Be sure that the stitches are slightly random in size and placement and that some overlap.

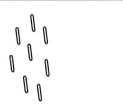

△ Fig. 124. Seed Stitch. Short single stitches used for detail filling or shading.

△ Fig. 125. Seed Stitch. Two very short stitches that come up in same hole and down beside each other, making a short broad stitch.

◁ Project #58: Strawberries. Full size pattern on page 140.

▷ *Fig. 127. Straight Stitch. Evergreen.*

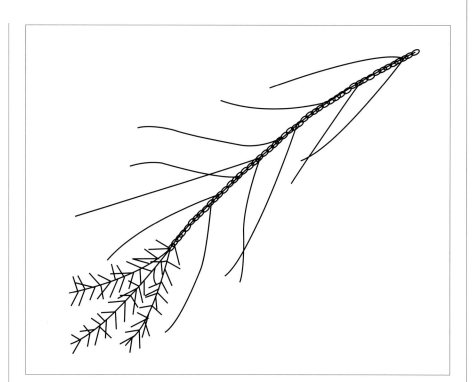

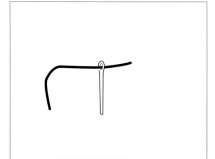

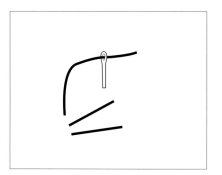

△ *Fig. 126a & b. Straight Stitch. Needle comes up at one end of stitch and goes down at other end; thread travels across surface.*

▷ *Project #59: Evergreen Needles. Full size pattern on page 125.*

FREE THREADS

Threads that hang free from the surface of the quilt can add an interesting texture to the work. Use threads that have body such as quilting thread or a heavier twisted thread.

PROJECT #60: FUCHSIA STAMENS

Thread a needle with a quilting thread in a color to match the upper flower petals and pull it through the eye to double it. Take a stitch up into the flower, leaving long tails showing. Take two stitches to secure the thread behind the center of the flower and come out to the front again. Leave 2" to 2½" (6 cm) of thread hanging free. Repeat the process with a single ply of thread, making a total of six stamens. Tie a small knot at the end of each thread and clip off the tails.

PROJECT #61: BLEEDING HEART

Prepare the bleeding heart block according to the techniques listed.

The "droplets" on the bleeding hearts are made with a loop of pearl cotton which hangs free from the surface. Begin and end the long loop stitch the same as a daisy stitch. Instead of couching over the end, use a fine thread to couch across the middle of the loop to hold it in place. (Fig. 128)

△ *Project #60: Fuchsia Stamens. See photos on pages 41 & 43. Full size pattern on page 115.*

△ *Fig. 128. Droplet Stitch.*

◁ *Project #61: Bleeding Heart. Full size pattern on page 141.*

◁ *Project #62: Follett House Flower. Wool thread example. Full size pattern on page 142.*

SPECIAL THREADS

Following are projects that offer an opportunity to experiment with special threads. Work with them to see what kind of surface texture or visual impact they can add to your appliqué. Check the suppliers listed at the end of the book. Their catalogs list many other types of threads that you might like to try.

WOOL

PROJECT #62: FOLLETT HOUSE FLOWER

This larger Follett House flower is worked in a manner similar to the stuffed flower in Project #7. Mark the outline and petal divisions of the flower onto a single flat piece of fabric. Pin the piece onto the background block. Appliqué a circle of contrasting color into place in the center of the flower, using wool as the appliqué thread. Stuff the center just before finishing the appliqué.

Use the same wool thread and a stem stitch to embroider the lines that divide the petals. Stuff each petal section individually, and if you like, use the wool thread to appliqué the outside edge closed.

SILK

PROJECT #63: SPIDER

Here is a spider for the web that you stitched earlier. Silk twist was used to give this spider some sheen and interesting texture. Use a single ply and a satin stitch to work the head and body, being careful to maintain the curved edges. Work the legs in stem stitch. (Fig. 129)

△ *Project #63: Spider.*
Silk thread example. See photo page 73. Full size pattern on page 131.

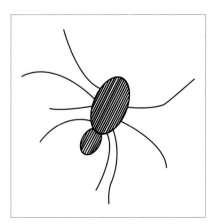

△ *Fig 129. Spider. Spider shown enlarged for detail. Full size block pattern on page 131.*

△ *Project #64: Heart Locket.*
Rayon thread example. See photo page 32. Full size pattern on page 109.

△ *Project # 65: Lyre.*
Metallic thread example. Full size pattern on page 143.

△ *Project # 66: Pearl Cotton Initial "A."*

▷ *Pearl Cotton Thread Example.*
Hobby Horse (detail). No pattern given.

RAYON

PROJECT #64: HEART LOCKET CHAIN

Refer to the heart locket in Project #14. Use a double ply of rayon floss and a chain stitch to add the chain to this block. The shine of this thread gives the look of real gold to the piece.

METALLIC

PROJECT #65: LYRE

A single ply of metallic thread and a chain stitch were used to add strings to the lyre. A variegated thread complements this blue fabric. Choose a thread color that will work best with your fabric palette.

PEARL COTTON

PROJECT #66: INITIAL "A"

Pearl cotton has many applications and always produces a beautiful texture. It was used as a filling stitch (textured satin) on the mane of this hobby horse.

In my little block, I have used a #5 pearl cotton and a stem stitch to outline a trapunto initial "A" to sign my work. You might like to do the same.

▷ *Flower Basket, 1991, 18"x 36"*
Made by Janet Hamilton.
Janet Hamilton made this basket of tulips and irises as part of her new album quilt. Techniques used included corded and padded appliqué, rolled buds, ruched iris beards, and outline embroidery.

GALLERY

The Shackelford Family Album Quilt, 1986-89, 80"x 90". Made by the author.
This album quilt contains designs that reflect the author's family life. Included are a family tree, a sailboat, a garden basket, favorite flowers, back yard birds and animals, and many other motifs that are personal and meaningful.

Those Our Hearts Are Fondest Of, 1988-91, 82"x 82". Made by the author.
This second album quilt designed and made by the author is a study in dimensional appliqué and includes many of the techniques presented in this book. While the style of the quilt maintains its traditional feeling, the designs are realistic, fresh, and new.

Etude: Anita, *1992, 21"x 25". Made by Glenda Clark.*
In music, an etude is a special composition designed to give practice in a special technique,
but often performed for its artistic merit. Glenda Clark found both to be true when she made
this basket of flowers.

Daffodils and Hummingbird, 1991, 23"x 23". Made by the author.
A design on a piece of Japanese porcelain was translated into this dimensional appliqué wall hanging. The ruched flowers and rolled bud are free-form. The hummingbird's rich colors were added with textured satin stitch embroidery over padded appliqué.

Folk Art Santa, 1991, 15"x 24". Made by Sheila Kennedy. Sheila's Santa carries a free-form walking stick and a lantern made with the padded reverse appliqué technique. Ruching and embroidery add dimension and detail to this design.

Victorian Santa, 1991, 15"x 23". Made by the author. This Santa wears a ruched beard and eyebrows and carries stuffed apples in his bag. The Christmas tree is worked with textured satin stitch and evergreen embroidery.

CHAPTER

5

PATTERNS

RUCHED FLOWERS – SMALL

Stems – ½" wide bias strip – Project #1, page 17

Leaves – flat appliqué

Leaf veins – stem stitch embroidery – Project #45, page 73, sewing thread

Flowers – small ruched flowers – Project #33, page 54

Flower centers – embroidered knots – Project #51 or Project #52, page 80

CHERRIES

Stem – ½" wide bias – corded stem – Project #2, page 19

Leaves – flat appliqué

Leaf stems and veins – stem stitch embroidery – Project #45, page 73, single ply floss

Cherries – padded appliqué – Project #5, page 22

Cherry stems – chain stitch embroidery – Project #47, page 75, double ply of floss

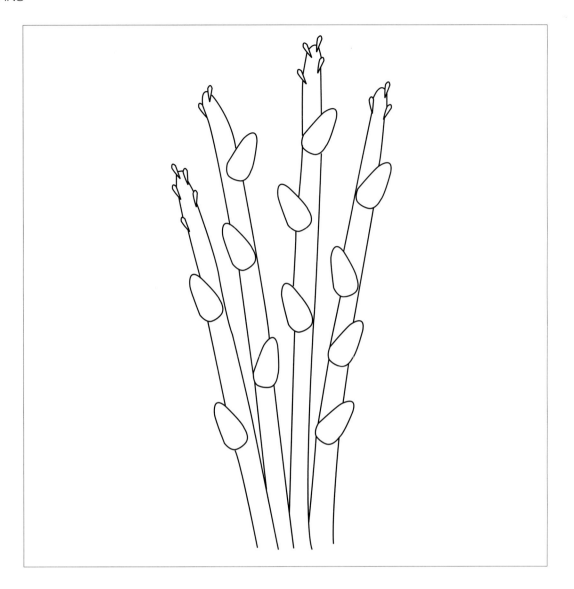

PUSSY WILLOW

Stems – ⅝" wide bias strip – corded stem – closed end – Project #3, page 20

Embroidered buds – daisy stitch – Project #57, page 85, double ply floss

Pussy Willow – unit appliqué – Project #18, page 37

GRAPES – STUFFED

Leaf stem – ½" wide bias – corded stem – Project #2, page 19

Grape stem – ¾" wide bias – free corded stem – Project #4, page 21

Main vine – ¾" wide bias – corded stem – Project #2, page 19

Leaf – flat appliqué

Leaf veins – stem stitch embroidery – Project #45, page 73, single ply floss

Grapes – stuffed appliqué – Project #6, page 23

Tendril – chain stitch embroidery – Project #47, page 75, single ply floss

FOLLETT HOUSE FLOWER

Stem – ¾" wide bias – flat stem – Project #1, page 17

Leaves – flat appliqué, may be embellished with reverse buttonhole stitch –
    Project #56, page 84, single ply floss

Flower – stuffed appliqué – Project #7, page 24

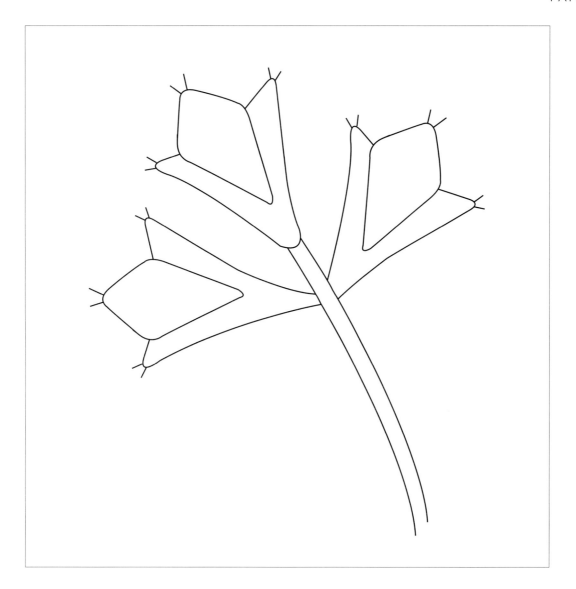

Flower Buds – stuffed

Stem – ⅝" wide bias – flat stem – Project #1, page 17

Calyx – flat appliqué

Bud – stuffed appliqué – Project #8, page 25

Embroidery – stem stitch embroidery – Project #45, page 73, sewing thread

ROSE

Embroidery details – stem stitch embroidery – Project #45, page 73, double ply floss

Stuffed appliqué – Project #9, page 26

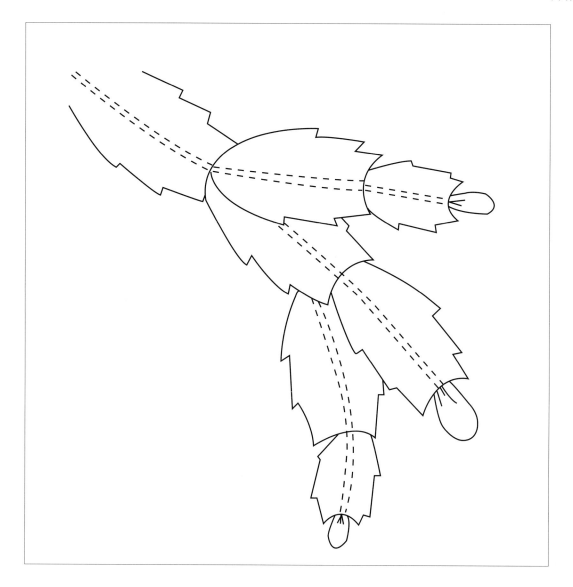

CHRISTMAS CACTUS

Christmas cactus – flat appliqué with channel trapunto – Project #10, page 27

Blossoms – gathered flower buds – Project #25, page 44, medium and large circles

STYLIZED FLOWER

Stem – ¾" wide bias – flat stem – Project #1, page 17

Leaf – flat appliqué

Flower – reverse appliqué – Project #11, page 28

STYLIZED BUD

Leaves – flat appliqué

Veins – stem stitch embroidery – Project #45, page 73, sewing thread

Buds – padded reverse appliqué – Project #12, page 29

MORNING GLORY

Leaf – flat appliqué

Veins – stem stitch embroidery – Project #45, page 73, sewing thread

Tendril – chain stitch embroidery – Project #47, page 75, single ply floss

Flower – padded appliqué with surface stitching – Project #13, page 31

Petal divisions – stem stitch embroidery – Project #45, page 73,
    machine embroidery weight thread worked through all layers

Flower center – straight stitch embroidery – Project #59, page 86, single ply floss.

Rolled bud – Project #26, page 45

HEART LOCKET

Heart – padded reverse appliqué – Project #12, page 29, center quilted through
to background block – Project #14, page 32

Chain – chain stitch embroidery – Project #47, page 75, two-ply rayon floss

VIOLETS

Stems – chain stitch embroidery – Project #47, page 75, double ply floss

Leaves – flat appliqué – one leaf-unit appliqué – Project #15, page 32

Leaf veins – stem stitch embroidery – Project #45, page 73, sewing thread

Violets – flat appliqué

Centers – Colonial knot – Project #52, page 80, double ply floss

Petal markings – straight stitch embroidery – Project #59, page 86, sewing thread

RIBBONS AND BOWS

Bow – unit appliqué – Project #16, page 34

Appliqué in place with running stitch, page 13

Center – stuffed appliqué – Project #6, page 23, blindstitch in place

CHICKADEE

Leaves – flat appliqué

Veins – stem stitch embroidery – Project #45, page 73, sewing thread

Chickadee – padded unit appliqué – Project #17, page 36

Evergreen – embroidery – Project #59, page 86

Berries – small berries – Project #28, page 48

Berry Stems – chain stitch – Project #47, page 75, double ply floss

DAISY

Stems – stem stitch embroidery – Project #45, page 73, double ply floss

Leaves – satin stitch embroidery – Project #48, page 76, double ply floss

Center – French or Colonial knots – Project #51, page 80, single ply floss

Daisies – embellished unit appliqué – Project #19, page 37

OAK LEAVES

Bottom leaf – flat appliqué

Top leaf – faced – Project #20, page 40

Stems – chain stitch embroidery – Project #47, page 75, double ply floss

Veins – stem stitch embroidery – Project #45, page 73, single ply floss

FUCHSIA

Branches – chain stitch embroidery – Project #47, page 75,
   one ply each of burgundy and green

Leaves – flat appliqué

Veins – stem stitch embroidery – Project #45, page 73, sewing thread

Buds – stuffed appliqué – Project #6, page 23

Flower caps – stuffed appliqué – Project #6, page 23

Petals – fused free-form – Project #21, page 40

Ruffled petals – Project #24, page 43

Stamens – free threads – Project #60, page 88

FLOWER BUD – FOLDED

Stem – ⅝" wide bias flat stem – Project #1, page 17

Leaves – flat appliqué

Flowers (calyx) – stuffed appliqué – Project #6, page 23

Centers – folded buds – Project #22, page 40, large and medium circles

PLEATED FLOWER

Leaves – flat appliqué

Stems – ⅝" wide bias flat stem – Project #1, page 17

Calyx – flat or stuffed appliqué – Project #6, page 23

Large flower – 2" x 5" bias – Project #23, page 42

Small flower – 1¾" x 3" bias – Project #23, page 42

GRAPES – FREE-FORM

Leaves – flat appliqué

Vine – chain stitch embroidery – Project #47, page 75, double ply floss

Tendrils – chain stitch embroidery – Project #47, page 75, single ply floss

Leaf veins – stem stitch embroidery – Project #45, page 73, single ply floss

Grapes – stuffed berries – Project #28, page 48, large circles

Blueberries

Branch and leaves – flat appliqué

Berries – Project #29, page 49, large and medium circles

LADYBUGS

Leaves – flat appliqué

Veins – stem stitch embroidery – Project #45, page 73, sewing thread

Stems – chain stitch embroidery – Project #47, page 75, sewing thread

Ladybug – free-form berry with embroidery details – Project #30, page 50

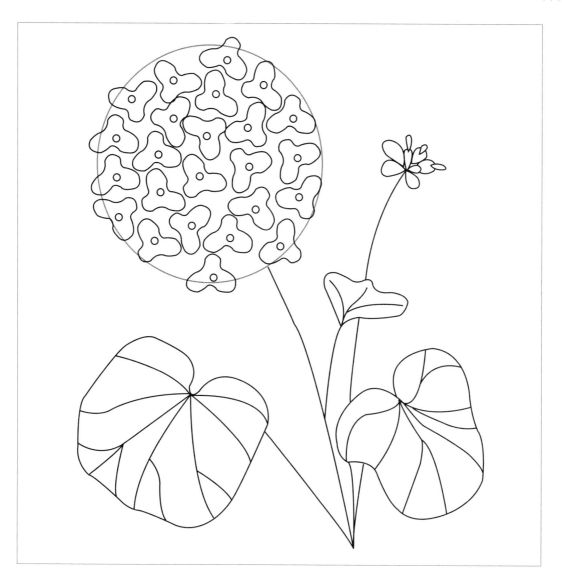

GERANIUM

Stems – ½" wide bias corded stem – Project #2, page 19

Leaves – flat appliqué

Veins – stem stitch embroidery – Project #45, page 73, sewing thread

Buds – small and medium berries – Project #28, page 48

Tiny blossoms – opening buds – Project #31, page 50

Geranium – composite or cluster-type flower – Project #35, page 56

LILY-OF-THE-VALLEY

Leaves – flat appliqué, one unit appliqué leaf – Project #15, page 32

Leaf veins – stem stitch embroidery – Project #45, page 73, sewing thread

Main stems – chain stitch embroidery – Project #47, page 75,
    sewing thread or one-ply floss

Small curved flower stems – stem stitch embroidery – Project #45, page 73,
    sewing thread or one-ply floss

Lily-of-the-Valley – bells – Project #32, page 51

Flower Buds – ruched

Leaf – flat appliqué

Small ruched flower – Project #33, page 54

Ruched buds – Project #34, page 55

Stems – stem stitch embroidery – Project #45, page 73, single ply floss

THISTLE

Stems – ½" wide bias flat stems – Project #1, page 17

Thistle head – ruching – Project #43, page 66

Thistle blossoms – textured satin stitch embroidery – Project #49, page 78,
    single ply of floss

Leaves – fused – Project #21, page 40

Butterfly – ruched – Project #36, page 56

Blindstitch butterfly into place around entire edge

Body – straight stitch embroidery – Project #59, page 86
    double ply of floss x 3 stitches

Antennae – stem stitch embroidery – Project #45, page 73,
    single ply of floss, knot at the end – Project #52, page 80

EVERGREEN

Main branch – chain stitch embroidery – Project #47, page 75,
one ply each dark green floss and rusty brown floss

Side stems – stem stitch embroidery – Project #45, page 73,
one ply medium green floss

Needles – straight stitch embroidery – Project #59, page 86,
one ply each dark green floss and light green floss

RUCHED FLOWER – TUFTED CENTER

Stems – ½" wide bias flat stems – Project #1, page 17

Leaves – flat appliqué

Flowers – ruched with tufted center – Project #38, page 60

RUCHED FLOWER – LARGE

Leaves – flat appliqué

Leaf Veins – stem stitch embroidery – Project #45, page 73, sewing thread

Flower – large flower with ruched edge – Project #39, page 60

Daffodil

Leaves – flat appliqué, one-unit appliqué – Projects #15, page 32

Stem – ⅝" wide bias corded stems – Project #2, page 19

Daffodil – Project #40, page 62

IRIS

Stem – ⅝" wide bias corded stems – Project #2, page 19

Calyx – stuffed appliqué – Project #6, page 23

Leaves – one flat appliqué, one folded – Project #15, page 32

Beards – ¼" x 2½" bias strip, ruched – Project #41, page 63
     ¼" x 3" bias strip, ruched – Project #41, page 63

Snowflakes

Snowflakes – Flat appliqué

Reverse appliqué small openings if you like

Outline embroidery – Project #44, page 72, extra fine thread

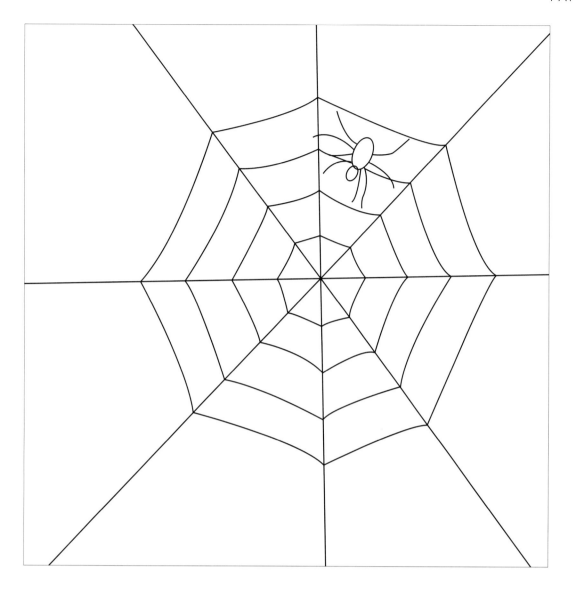

SPIDER WEB

Web – stem stitch embroidery – Project #45, page 73,
   single ply sewing thread or machine embroidery weight thread, white, light gray

Spider – body – satin stitch embroidery – Project #48, page 76, single ply silk twist
   legs – stem stitch embroidery – Project #45, page 73, single ply silk twist –
      Project #63, page 89

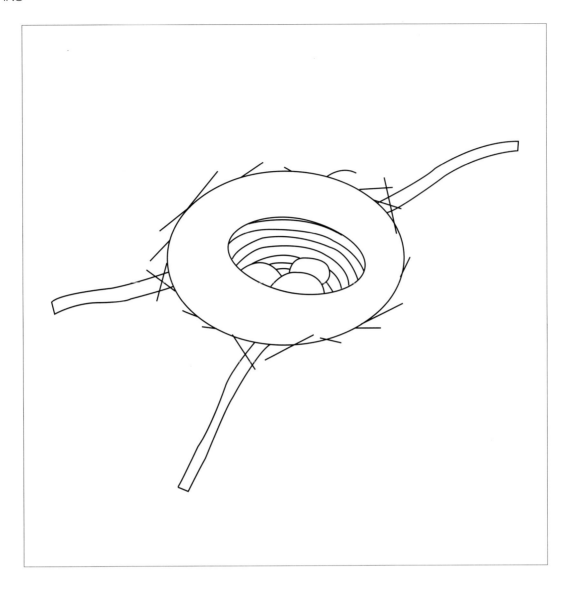

BIRD'S NEST

Branches – ½" wide bias corded stem – Project #2, page 19

Interior lines of nest – couched – Project #46, page 74,
   crewel wool couched with sewing thread.

Eggs – stuffed appliqué – Project #6, page 23

Rim of nest – long straight stitch embroidery – Project #59, page 86,
   follow contours of nest.

Hibiscus

Leaves – flat appliqué

Leaf veins – stem stitch embroidery – Project #45, page 73, sewing thread

Petals – flat appliqué, outline embroidery – Project #44, page 72, sewing thread

Stem – chain stitch embroidery – Project #47, page 75,
    one ply each red and green floss

Pistil – chain stitch embroidery – Project #47, page 75, two-ply floss

Stamens – straight stitch embroidery – Project #59, page 86, single ply floss,
    knots at ends – Project #51 or #52, page 80

Butterfly – satin stitch

Branches – stem stitch embroidery – Project #45, page 73, single ply floss

Butterfly – wing spots – outline embroidery – Project #44, page 72, single ply floss
    edges – satin stitch embroidery – Project #48, page 76, double ply floss
    edge spots – French or Colonial knots – Project #52, page 80, double ply floss
    body – textured satin stitch – Project #49, page 78, double ply floss
    antennae – stem stitch embroidery – Project #45, page 73, single ply floss
        daisy stitch at end

Add tufts to background branches if you like – Project #27, page 46

HUMMINGBIRD

Bird – single piece of fabric – padded appliqué – Project #5, page 22

Head, throat, back, tail – textured satin stitch embroidery – Project #50, page 78,
    single ply floss worked in surface fabric only

Eye – satin stitch embroidery – Project #48, page 76

Beak – stem stitch embroidery (2 lines) – Project #45, page 73, single ply floss

Outline wings if desired – outline stitch embroidery – Project #44, page 72,
    single ply floss or sewing thread

Yarrow

Main stem – chain stitch embroidery – Project #47, page 75, double ply floss

Small stems – chain stitch embroidery – Project #47, page 75, single ply floss

Leaves – flat appliqué

Leaf veins – stem stitch embroidery – Project #45, page 73, sewing thread

A good place to put your caterpillar

Yarrow blossom – Colonial knot – Project #52, page 80, double ply floss

DAYLILY

Leaves – flat appliqué

Stem – ½" bias corded stem – Project #2, page 19

Petals – flat appliqué, may pad forward one

Petal veins – stem stitch embroidery – Project #45, page 73, double ply floss

Pistil – chain stitch embroidery – Project #47, page 75, single ply floss

Stamens – stem stitch embroidery – Project #45, page 73, single ply floss

Anthers – Bullion knots – Project #53, page 82, double ply floss

FOLK ART BIRD

Branch – 1" wide bias flat stem – Project #1, page 17, running stitch appliqué

Bird – flat appliqué

Wing – buttonhole stitch – Project #54, page 83, double ply floss

Eye – French or Colonial knot – Project #52, page 80, double ply floss

Legs – stem stitch embroidery – Project #45, page 73, single ply floss

FORGET-ME-NOTS

Leaves – flat appliqué

Veins – stem stitch embroidery – Project #45, page 73, sewing thread

Stems – chain stitch embroidery – Project #47, page 75, double ply floss

Tiny leaves – daisy stitch – Project #57, page 85, double ply floss

Flowers – daisy stitch – Project #57, page 85, double ply floss

Centers – Colonial knot – Project #52, page 80, double ply floss

Buds – Colonial knot – Project #52, page 80, double ply floss

STRAWBERRIES

Leaves – flat appliqué

Veins – stem stitch embroidery – Project #45, page 73, sewing thread

Main stems – chain stitch embroidery – Project #47, page 75, double ply floss

Small stems – stem stitch embroidery – Project #45, page 73, single ply floss

Berries – padded appliqué – Project #5, page 22

Caps – daisy stitch – Project #57, page 85

Seeds – seed stitch embroidery – Project #58, page 86, worked through all layers

Blossom – composite flower – Project #35, page 56, ½" silk ribbon

Blossom center – tuft – Project #27, page 46

Bud – small berry gathered and put down on its side – Project #28, page 48

BLEEDING HEART

Branch – chain stitch embroidery – Project #47, page 75, two colors of floss

Leaves – flat appliqué

Veins – stem stitch embroidery – Project #45, page 73, sewing thread

Stems – stem stitch embroidery – Project #45, page 73, single ply floss

Flowers – stuffed appliqué – Project #6, page 23

Drops – loop of pearl cotton – couched in center with sewing thread –
    Project #61, page 88

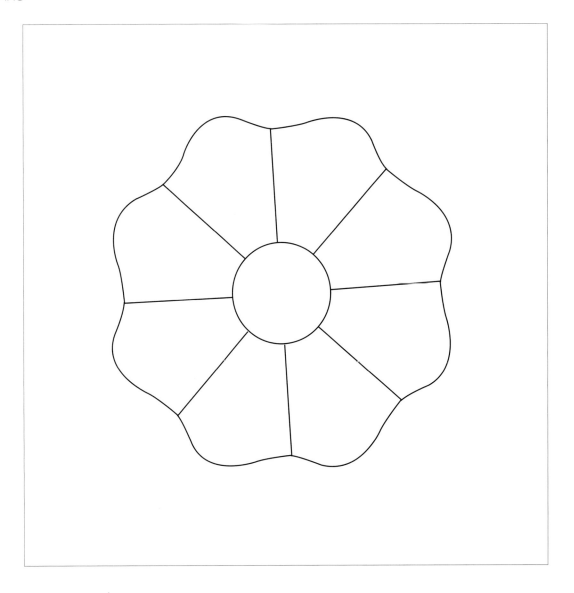

FOLLETT HOUSE FLOWER – WOOL

Flower – stuffed appliqué – Project #7, page 24,
   petal lines worked with stem stitch embroidery – Project #45, page 73,
   single ply crewel wool – Project #62, page 89

Center – stuffed appliqué – Project #6, page 23, stitched in place with crewel wool

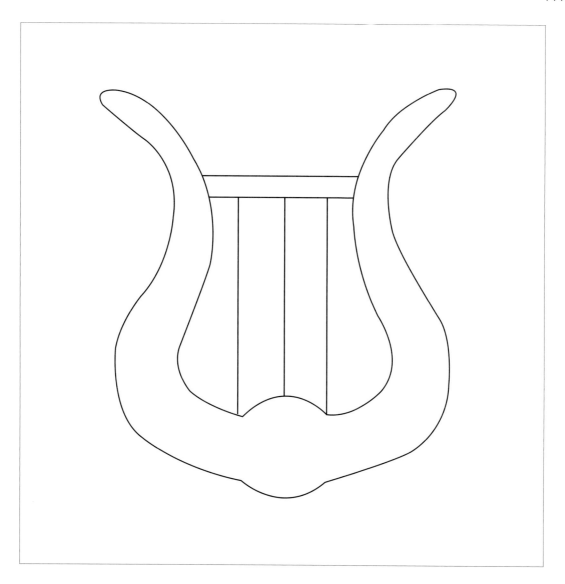

LYRE

Lyre – flat appliqué
Strings – chain stitch embroidery – Project #47, page 75,
    variegated metallic thread; Project #65, page 90

REFERENCES

SOURCES OF PRODUCTS

Please check with your local quilt shop to see if they stock or are able to order needed supplies for you. If not, this list of mail-order sources may be helpful.

PRODUCTS AVAILABLE AT:

CLOTHILDE
1909 S W FIRST AVE.
FORT LAUDERDALE, FL
33315-2100

Fasturn®
Stuff-it®
Markers
½" sequin pins
Fray Check®
Needle gripper
Clover®, Piecemaker®, and
John James® needles

PRODUCTS AVAILABLE AT:

THE MAGIC NEEDLE
PO BOX 144
BIDDEFORD, ME 04005

DMC® flower thread
Pearl cotton
Silk, rayon threads
Metallic thread

PRODUCTS AVAILABLE AT:

NORDIC NEEDLE
1314 GATEWAY DR.
FARGO, ND 58103
www.nordicneedle.com

DMC® cotton floss
Pearl cotton
Crewel wool
Metallic Threads
Linen, silk, rayon thread

PRODUCTS AVAILABLE AT:

OSAGE COUNTY QUILT FACTORY
400 WALNUT
OVERBROOK, KS 66524

Piecemaker® and John James®
    sharps for appliqué
Procion® dyes
Synthrapol®
Fasturn®
Marking pencils

NEEDLE NECESSITIES, INC
7211 GARDEN GROVE BLVD., #BC
GARDEN GROVE, CA 92841
www.needlenecessities.com

PRODUCTS AVAILABLE AT:

THIMBLE WORKS
BOX 462
BUCYRUS, OH 44820
www.thimbleworks.com

RucheMark™ ruching guides

PRODUCTS AVAILABLE AT:

WEB OF THREAD
3240 LONE OAK ROAD
SUITE 124
PADUCAH, KY 42003
www.webofthread.com

Sulky® rayon threads
Silk ribbon
Metallic thread and ribbon
Cording and braid for couching
Burmalana® acrylic thread

CUSTOM HOUSE OF NEEDLE ARTS LLC
154 WEIR ST
GLASTONBURY, CT 06033
www.gumnutyarns.com

STITCH WITH THE EMBROIDERER'S GUILD
PO BOX 42B
EAST MOLESEY
SURREY
KT8 9BB UK
www.embroiderersguild.org.uk

For workshop information, contact

ANITA SHACKELFORD
1539 FAIRVIEW AVE.
BUCYRUS, OH 44820

REFERENCE READING

Anderson, Faye. *Appliqué Designs: My Mother Taught Me to Sew*. Paducah, KY: American Quilter's Society, 1990.

Benson, Jeanne. *The Art and Technique of Appliqué*. McLeon, VA: EPM Publications, Inc., 1991.

Buckley, Karen. *From Basics to Binding: A Complete Guide*. Paducah, KY: American Quilter's Society, 1992.

Bullard, Lacy Folmar and Betty Jo Shiell. *Chintz Quilts: Unfading Glory*. Tallahassee, FL: Serendipity Publishers, 1983.

Coats and Clark. *100 Embroidery Stitches*. New York, NY, 1964.

Dietrick, MiMi. *Baltimore Bouquets*. Bothell, WA: That Patchwork Place, 1991.

Doak, Carol. *Quiltmaker's Guide: Basics and Beyond*. Paducah, KY: American Quilter's Society, 1992.

Finley, Ruth E. *Old Patchwork Quilts and the Women Who Made Them*. Charles T. Branford Co., 1929.

Fritz, Laura Lee. *Art of Hand Appliqué*. Paducah, KY: American Quilter's Society, 1990.

Hall, Carrie A. and Rose Kretsinger. *The Romance of the Patchwork Quilt in America*. Crown Publishers, Inc., 1935.

Hatcher, Irma Gail. *Conway Album Quilt*. San Marcos, CA: ASN Publishing Company, Inc., 1993.

Hinson, Dolores. *A Quilter's Companion*. New York, NY: Arco Publishing Company, Inc., 1973.

Ickis, Marguerite. *The Standard Book of Quiltmaking and Collecting*. New York, NY: Dover Publications, Inc., 1949.

Kimball, Jeana. *Red and Green: An Appliqué Tradition*. Bothell, WA: That Patchwork Place, Inc., 1990.

Marston and Cunningham. *American Beauties: Rose & Tulip Quilts*. Paducah, KY: American Quilter's Society, 1988.

Montano, Judith. *Crazy Quilt Odyssey*. Martinez, CA: C&T Publishing, 1991.

Nelson, Cyril and Carter Houck. *Treasury of American Quilts*. Crown Publishers, Inc., 1982.

Sienkiewicz, Elly. *Baltimore Beauties and Beyond: Studies in Classic Album Quilt Appliqué*, Volume 1. Lafayette, CA: C&T Publishing, 1989.

Sienkiewicz, Elly. *Appliqué 12 Easy Ways!* Lafayette, CA: C & T Publishing, 1991.

Sinema, Laurene. *Appliqué! Appliqué!! Appliqué!!!* Gualala, CA: The Quilt Digest Press, 1992.

Sunset Books. *Quilting Patchwork and Appliqué*. Menlo Park, CA: Lane Publishing Co., 1973.

Webster, Marie. *Quilts: Their Story and How to Make Them*. Detroit, MI: The Gale Research Company, 1972, Doubleday, Page and Co., 1915.

Wilson, Erica. *Crewel Embroidery*. New York, NY: Charles Scribner's Sons, 1962.

PATTERN INDEX

TECHNIQUE INDEX

PHOTO INDEX

ABOUT THE AUTHOR

Anita Shackelford has been making quilts since 1967 and teaching since 1980. She has taught in her home, for adult education, for shops and guilds across the US, and for AQS and NQA during their annual shows.

Anita has been a member of the National Quilting Association (NQA) since 1982 and is currently serving as membership chairman. She is a charter member of the American Quilter's Society (AQS) and also belongs to the American Quilt Study Group, and Country Crossroads Quilters in Bucyrus, Ohio.

Anita's quilts have won awards in shows across the United States, including six Best of Shows and several for technical excellence. Two of her quilts have received the Mary Krickbaum Award for best hand quilting at a National Quilting Association show.

The focus of her work is on dimensional appliqué and fine hand quilting. She enjoys using and teaching nineteenth century techniques, combined with her own designs, to create today's album quilts. She is also a NQA certified quilt judge and has been involved in judging shows at local, regional, and national levels.

OTHER AQS BOOKS

This is only a small selection of the books available from the American Quilter's Society. AQS books are known worldwide for timely topics, clear writing, beautiful color photos, and accurate illustrations and patterns. The following books are available from your local bookseller, quilt shop, or public library.

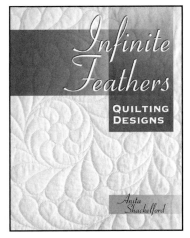

#6072 . . . .$25.95

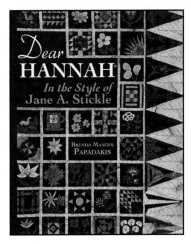

#6296 . . . .$25.95

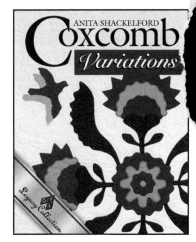

#5706 . . . .$18.95

#6211 . . . .$19.95

#6205 . . . .$24.95

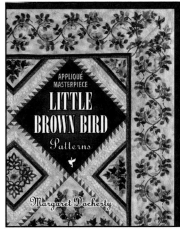

#5338 . . . .$21.95

#5763 . . . .$21.95

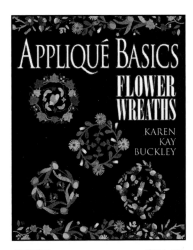

#5335 . . . .$21.95

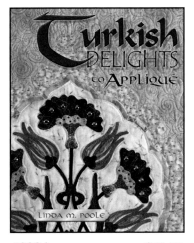

#6004 . . . .$22.95

LOOK for these books nationally. **CALL** or **VISIT** our website at www.AQSquilt.com

1-800-626-5420